From Resurrection to New Creation

From
Resurrection
to
New Creation

A First Journey in Christian Theology

Michael W. Pahl

 CASCADE *Books* · Eugene, Oregon

FROM RESURRECTION TO NEW CREATION
A First Journey in Christian Theology

Cascade Books
An Imprint of Wipf and Stock Publishers
199 W. 8th Ave., Suite 3
Eugene, OR 97401

www.wipfandstock.com

ISBN 13: 978-1-602899-259-1

Cataloguing-in-Publication data:

Pahl, Michael W.

From resurrection to new creation : a first journey in Christian theology / Michael W. Pahl.

xiv + 132 p. ; 20 cm. Includes bibliographical references and indexes.

ISBN 13: 978-1-602899-259-1

1. Theology, Doctrinal. 2. Theology—History I. Title.

BT65.P3 2010

Manufactured in the U.S.A.

To my children:
Amelia, Michael, Matthew, and Adalynne.

May you always grow in the grace and knowledge
of our crucified and risen Lord Jesus Christ.

Contents

Preface

THIS BOOK IS a journey through the essential truths of the Christian faith—but it is not your typical survey of Christian theology.

The structure may be the first clue that something is different. Such surveys or introductions are sometimes arranged around the conventional "heads of doctrine" in logical order, an arrangement of systematic theology often categorized under such "-ologies" as Bibliology (theology of Scripture), Theology (God), Anthropology (humanity), Hamartiology (sin), Christology (Christ), Soteriology (salvation), Pneumatology (the Spirit), Ecclesiology (the church), and Eschatology (last things). This book, by contrast, moves from Resurrection to Creation, with chapters on Crucifixion, Son, Gospel, Father, and Spirit in between. This unusual arrangement reflects the central contention of the book: that the resurrection of the crucified Jesus was both the ground and the center of earliest Christian theology and practice, and so should it also be for Christians today. All distinctively Christian theology and practice should begin by grappling with the resurrection of the crucified Jesus, and all distinctively Christian theology and practice should grow out of the reality—and be centered on the reality—that the crucified Jesus has been resurrected from the dead.

This points to another feature of this book which sets it apart from at least some other surveys of Christian doctrine. In these pages I attempt to describe how the essential truth claims of historically orthodox Christianity are themselves grounded in prior historical events and ideas and have developed out of those events and ideas. The doctrine of the Trinity, for example, did not suddenly appear fully formed in the fourth century AD, but grew out of the life and worship of the earliest Christians as they wrestled with the full significance of the reality that God had raised the crucified Jesus from the dead. In other words, the New Testament authors were themselves "doing theology" as they explored the new terrain laid out before them in light of Jesus' resurrection. Thus, the Trinity and other distinctive Christian doctrines and practices are, in a real sense, first a matter of history before they are a dogma of theology.

And this in turn leads to another characteristic of this book: the desire to bring biblical studies and dogmatic theology closer together, as these are too often divorced in theological study. While there is tremendous value in studying the texts of the canonical writings and the ideas of the biblical authors for purely historical purposes, for the Christian there must always be a further theological aim in doing so, to discern how we as Christians should think and live in our own day. And, while there is great merit in exploring the ideas of traditional and contemporary Christianity for wholly doctrinal reasons, for the Christian there must always be an attempt to ground such ideas in the historically conditioned texts and events which we claim to hold as authoritative for our faith. In this book I endeavor to do these very things through a biblical theological approach—albeit in a rather cursory and limited way. But of course that is what makes this book a survey and not a full-blown academic monograph. It is, if you will, an initial survey of the terrain of Christian theology, not a detailed mapping.

In spite of these potentially complex underlying intentions and perspectives, this book is still an introductory orientation (or perhaps, for some, a re-orientation) to essential Christian theology. One could think of it as an overview of Christian theology through the lenses of biblical and narrative theology, or perhaps as a New Testament theology in miniature. It is a first journey in Christian theology which attempts to re-trace that first journey taken by the earliest Christians. As such it will likely be most useful for beginning theological students in a Christian context, pastors and others involved in vocational Christian ministry, and interested laypeople who wish to understand and express their Christian faith better or differently. In light of this I have made the decision to avoid notes throughout the book apart from direct biblical references; rather, key biblical passages and other helpful resources which relate to the themes and ideas of each chapter are noted at the end of the chapter. In addition, one will find questions at the beginning and end of each chapter which may be used to help individual readers or groups to reflect on the content of the chapter, and I have provided a glossary at the end of the book which gives a brief definition or description of the more technical terms used in the book. Nevertheless, despite these indications of the introductory nature of the book, there is no reason why it should be unduly restricted in its audience, and I do hope it will prove useful to any and all who have an interest in the origins and essence of Christian faith and life.

☙

One editorial comment deserves mention here. As will be amply illustrated throughout this book, I see all language about God as analogous. That is, we as finite human beings can only speak about an infinite divine being in images, metaphors, similes, and the like. This includes the names we ascribe to God and the pronouns we use to refer to God. God is beyond the human gender categories of "male" and "female," and yet God is a personal being who encompasses the positive attributes typically associated with each human gender—both male and female are created in God's image. Thus, the pronoun "it" wrongly de-personalizes God, the pronoun "she" simply transfers the problems of "he," and I judge constructions such as "he/she" or "s/he" to be too awkward and alternating between "he" and "she" to be too confusing. I have therefore tried to minimize the use of pronouns to refer to God, but when necessary I have used the masculine pronouns for God simply as a grammatical convention.

☙

Any book—even a short one such as this—is the cumulative result of innumerable personal influences, and so some expressions of thanks are necessary.

First and foremost, my wife Larissa and my children (to whom this book is dedicated) deserve more thanks than I can muster. They not only put up with my extra hours at the computer to work on projects such as this book, but they also see when I fail to live up to my own Christian ideals, when I lose my way in my own exploration of Christian faith and life, and they inevitably respond with grace and mercy.

I would like to thank Wipf & Stock for taking this book into their publishing fold, and Christian Amondson in particular for providing excellent editorial leadership through to the completion of the project.

Thanks are also due to the many teachers I have had—both in person and by proxy through their writings—who have directly or indirectly shaped my thinking on Christian theology and the New Testament: personal teachers such as Mark Goodacre, Chuck Guth, and Ken Radant, and proxy teachers such as Richard Bauckham, Gordon Fee, Michael Gorman, Richard Hays, George Ladd, Howard Marshall, Scot McKnight, Jürgen Moltmann, N. T. Wright, and many others. Their influence—particularly the influence of those I have just named, especially through the writings I've highlighted in the book—can be seen on nearly every page.

I am also grateful for the many colleagues and hundreds of students I have had over the years in my teaching roles, especially those who journeyed with me toward a deeper reflection on Christian theology and practice during my time at Prairie Bible College (1998–2008). The ideas represented in this book have also made their way into sermons and series in various churches in many settings. Thank you especially to the good folks at Mount Olive Evangelical Free Church and Lendrum Mennonite Brethren Church for encouraging me in these ideas and for journeying the Christian faith and life together with me.

Finally, I owe a large debt of gratitude to friends and colleagues who reviewed earlier drafts of this book: Mike Bird,

Mike Gorman, TC Ham, Daniel Kirk, Scot McKnight, David Miller, and my brother Steven Pahl. The book is certainly better for their labor, and their comments have undoubtedly delivered me from some egregious problems and errors. However, in spite of their best efforts, there are just as undoubtedly some such problems and errors which remain—an accomplishment for which I alone can take the credit.

Michael Pahl
Advent Sunday 2009

Prologue

The Apostles' Gospel Creed

NEARLY TWO THOUSAND years ago, Jesus of Nazareth was crucified outside Jerusalem between two convicted brigands, deserted by most of his friends, apparently forsaken even by his God.

But within a few days, strange things began to happen. Jesus' closest followers, several women who had supported him and others who had been his disciples, claimed to have seen Jesus alive. James, Jesus' brother, who had once been skeptical of Jesus and his chosen vocation, also professed to having seen Jesus. And finally, even a violent persecutor of these followers of Jesus, an up-and-coming Pharisee named Saul, maintained that he had seen the crucified Jesus alive, resurrected by God.

Twenty-five years later, Saul, or Paul as he was now known, described these events—Jesus' death and resurrection —as "gospel" or "good news," the most important of all news, news which ensured "salvation" for those who believed in it and stood firm upon it, news which all these resurrection witnesses uniformly proclaimed:

I want to remind you of the gospel I preached to you, which you received and on which you have taken your stand. By this gospel you are saved . . . For what I received I passed on to you as of first importance:

> that Christ died for our sins according to the Scriptures,
> that he was buried,
> that he was raised on the third day according to the Scriptures,
> and that he appeared to Peter, and then to the Twelve. . . .

Whether, then, it is I or they, this is what we preach, and this is what you believed.

(1 Corinthians 15:1–11)

1

Resurrection

Before you read . . .

- What comes to mind when you think of the word "resurrection"?
- Why do you believe in Jesus' resurrection?
- How would you describe the significance of Jesus' resurrection from the dead?

IN THE BEGINNING God raised Jesus from the dead.

Of course, Christians affirm that God had acted long before this, creating the universe "in the beginning" and working throughout human history to achieve his purposes. God had, according to the sacred narratives of the Jewish Scriptures, chosen a people to shine the light of his creative power, perfect justice, and faithful love to all the nations of the earth. Through this power, justice, and love God had sustained the chosen people of ancient Israel through slavery and wars and exiles and oppression.

A great deal had also happened to Jesus before this. He had grown up in Nazareth, much like any other Jewish boy of his era, learning and living the Law of Moses, loving and laughing and lamenting within the tight weave of kinship and friendship in that small Galilean village. He had left home in his early thirties, taking up what he sensed to be a prophetic call to proclaim throughout the towns and villages of Israel that God's sovereign and saving rule had arrived. He had become known as a teacher, a miracle-worker, even a messiah—as well as a glutton, a drunkard, and a keeper of the most unseemly company. He had pushed the buttons of the Jewish religious establishment in Jerusalem and caught the attention of the Roman political authorities in Caesarea, eventually being charged with blasphemy by the former and sedition by the latter. And he had, as a result, been crucified on a crude Roman cross outside the walls of Jerusalem like a common criminal.

Yet for the earliest followers of Jesus his resurrection from the dead was a new beginning, the vindication of their teacher, their prophet, their miracle-working Messiah. Jesus' resurrection was the end of his pre-determined end, the beginning of a promised new existence. For the earliest followers of Jesus, his resurrection from the dead was a fresh start in God's action in the world, even the beginning of a new act of creation. By raising Jesus from the dead, transforming him to a new life untouched by sin and death, God initiated a new era in the history of humanity and the world.

This event was also the beginning of a new way of thinking for the first followers of Jesus, a new way of perceiving reality and knowing truth. The resurrection of Jesus was, in the sharpest sense of the term, an "apocalyptic" event; that is, it turned the world upside down and so changed forever the way in which the world must be viewed. Indeed, the central contention of this book is that the resurrection of the crucified Jesus is the ground and center of all truly Christian thought and action, both the source and the focus of all belief and behavior that can be called authentically Christian. The earliest Christian theology and practice grew out of the reality—and was centered on the reality—that the crucified Jesus had been resurrected from the dead. Or, to put this another way, the resurrection of the crucified Jesus was both the starting place and the compass for the first followers of Jesus in their journey to understand God and God's work in the world and to live out God's purposes for them, and so should it also be for Christians today.

∞

The concept of "resurrection" in its fullest form was a relatively recent development in Jewish thought in Jesus' day, having evolved from earlier biblical hopes into a well-developed doctrine by the time of Jesus. The age-old stories of the Israelites and their surrounding cultures had long played with "life-after-death" motifs. The never-ending cycle of life to death to new life was felt in the rhythms of changing seasons and the cadence of human existence, and this cycle echoed in the mythological deeds of gods and goddesses. Resuscitations were not unheard of in the ancient world, with claims of the dead or near-dead being revived even through miracle or magic. And some sort of existence after death was assumed by most people, whether as a pale shadow of one's earthly self or as a disembodied soul freed from its earthly cage.

But the bold idea of resurrection was not like any of these. Unlike mythic stories of the gods in a never-ending cycle of life, resurrection was for real people, flesh-and-blood men and women and children who had actually lived and died. Unlike claims of resuscitations, resurrection was forever; a person resuscitated, however miraculously so, would still die again, but the future resurrection of the dead would involve a transformed existence untouched by death. And unlike popular ideas of continued existence after death, resurrection was not just for souls but also for bodies—a genuinely holistic human existence.

By Jesus' day, the significance of this Jewish concept of resurrection could be summed up in two ideas: *renewal* and *vindication*. Resurrection was an eschatological event; that is, it was seen as a mark of the end of the present age and the beginning of the eternal new age, the time of the eschaton. So, for those Jews who believed in it, "resurrection" was bound up with such other ideas as "new creation," "kingdom of God," "final judgment," and, in many quarters, the promised "Messiah." The resurrection of the righteous, those who had faithfully maintained their covenant relationship with God, was vitally connected to the promise of God's renewal of creation. In this eternal new age God was to reverse the curse of sin imposed on Adam's children, turning death and hostility, pain and futility, into life and peace. In the Messiah-wrought kingdom of God, the resurrected people of God would experience renewed life in a new creation.

Resurrection was also about vindication. Death is the ultimate oppression of humanity, the final act of shame and condemnation in the tragedy of human life. Death by crucifixion especially emphasized this. The Romans were cruelly capable in crucifying the unwanted, but crucifixion was more than simply an efficient means of execution. Those who were crucified had been convicted of the most heinous crimes in the Empire; they were stripped of their clothing and displayed prominently on public roads outside city gates; they were the outcasts of empire, the non-citizens and conquered peoples. Everything about crucifixion reinforced the exalted status of the Roman Empire and emphasized the lowly status of the crucified as the condemned, the shamed, the oppressed. The Jewish hope of the resurrection was an expectation that all this would be reversed: the unjustly condemned would be justified, the wrongly shamed would be honored, and the cruelly oppressed would be liberated. At the resurrection of the righteous, God's people would finally be vindicated before the world.

Jesus' resurrection was just such a vindication. As Peter's Pentecost sermon in Acts states it, the religious and political rulers of the day might have condemned Jesus on a cross, "but God raised him from the dead" (Acts 2:24). By raising Jesus from the dead, God had overturned the verdicts of blasphemy and sedition by which Jesus was condemned; God had justified Jesus, declaring before the world that he was in fact innocent of all charges, that his kingdom teachings and actions were in fact true expressions of God's will in the world. By raising Jesus from the dead, God had honored Jesus, turning the shame of his crucifixion into the glory of an exalted status in God's presence. And by raising the oppressed and marginalized Jesus from the dead, God liberated him and brought him into the very center of God's purposes in the world.

Jesus' resurrection was also a renewal. For Jesus the curse of sin was decisively reversed, with death, hostility, pain, and apparent futility transformed into life and peace. Jesus was raised to new creation life, forever untouched by sin and death.

As Peter's Pentecost sermon goes on to say, he was "[freed] from the agony of death, because it was impossible for death to keep its hold on him" (Acts 2:24). Or, as Paul describes, Jesus' resurrection involved a transformation from dishonor, weakness, corruptibility, and mortality, to glory, power, incorruptibility, and immortality—through Jesus' resurrection "death has been swallowed up in victory" (1 Corinthians 15:54). Jesus became the first person to fully experience *shalom*, the "peace" or wholeness and harmony of human existence eternally blessed by God. He became the first person to finally fulfill the promise of *imago Dei*, the royal stamp of the "image of God" on his beloved human children and the mark of God's call to extend his loving rule throughout creation.

These sorts of thoughts are hinted at in the very early Christian description of Jesus' resurrection as "on the third day" (1 Corinthians 15:4). The "third day" was, after all, the awaited time of God's action on behalf of his people: the divine deliverance of Abraham's promised, beloved son Isaac from certain sacrifice occurred "on the third day" (Genesis 22:4); it was "on the third day" that God met Moses before the gathered people of Israel on Mount Sinai to give the Law and establish the nation (Exodus 19:16); Hezekiah's restoration from the edge of death to full health and purity was to be acknowledged in the Temple "on the third day" (2 Kings 20:5); Hosea's promised restoration of the people of Israel from oppression and exile would take place "on the third day" (Hosea 6:2). And so it was only appropriate that God raised Jesus from the dead "on the third day," finally bringing about the long-awaited renewal and vindication to creation and humanity.

Such confident expectation of divine renewal and vindication through resurrection, patterned after Jesus' attitude toward his own future and based upon Jesus' resurrection from
the dead, is summed up in a significant biblical word: *hope*.

CR

Of course, all this assumes that Jesus was in fact "raised from
the dead." But how do we know that he was? On what basis can
we believe in Jesus' resurrection? Many have tried to "prove"
Jesus' resurrection on historical or logical grounds. Nearly as
many have tried to "disprove" it on the same grounds. Both
groups, it seems to me, badly miss the point.

"The scandal of the cross" is generally well known to
Christians. The idea that the Messiah, the king from David's
dynasty, would be crucified, accursed by God and humans,
was outrageous to first-century Jews. The idea that a king, a
son of the gods, would be crucified on a Roman cross was foolishness to first-century Gentiles (1 Corinthians 1:22–24). One
does not hear the phrase "the scandal of the resurrection"—
or, to keep the analogy, "the scandal of the empty tomb"—yet
there is certainly something scandalous about the claim that
Jesus of Nazareth was "raised on the third day" (1 Corinthians
15:4). Christianity's most foundational theological claim is
also a historical claim: something happened to the corpse
of a Galilean man on an April Sunday morning nearly two
thousand years ago. Thus the nature of the claim is such that
it *demands* historical investigation. Yet the nature of the claim
is such that it *defies* historical investigation. This is the scandal
of the empty tomb.

All sound historical research rests on three basic pillars:
the principles of *probability*, *analogy*, and *correlation*. The

principle of probability is essentially a recognition that history is not like the mathematical or empirical sciences. A historian cannot produce a tight series of logical proofs, nor can he or she conduct a controlled experiment which can be directly observed and repeated as necessary. The events of ancient history are past, never to be observed again, only accessible through incomplete written reminisces and partial material remains—sources which must be carefully and critically sifted as to their authenticity and reliability. Thus all judgments concerning historical events are necessarily cautious, at best describing a high probability and not an absolute certainty. The *principle of analogy* recognizes that we can only understand a specific historical event through comparison with similar historical events. This is not to deny the uniqueness of historical events—indeed, each and every natural or human event really is unique—but rather this principle simply recognizes that every historical event has relevant points of comparison with other events in history or today. The *principle of correlation* holds that every historical event is the effect of natural, historical causes, and that every event in turn is the cause of subsequent effects. Events in history do not happen in isolation from everything around them; rather they are integrally related to their particular historical setting. These three principles are so commonsensical that to dispute them would be to discard all reason in doing historical research.

But the claim that Jesus of Nazareth was "raised from the dead on the third day," transformed to an immortal bodily existence untouched by sin and death, does not sit well with these principles of sound historical methodology. This resurrection claim is in fact a claim that an utterly unique event has taken place, without any analogy in history. Claims of dead people being resuscitated even long after their death simply do not fit, nor do claims of visionary experiences of disembodied spirits. These sorts of claims are just not what is going on in the New Testament claim that Jesus was "resurrected." What's more, no Christian would claim that God's resurrection of Jesus was directly caused by any person or event or anything else in the historical situation. Rather, the Christian claim is that the resurrection of Jesus was solely a divine incursion into human history, without historical cause though with great historical effect. And this claim demands a response that sits outside of a clinical spectrum of plausibility to probability; it does not call for a verdict of "highly probable" or even "irrefutably certain," but rather it calls forth a deep conviction of faith. A historical event without analogy, without correlation, without cautious statements of probability? Such is the scandal of the empty tomb.

Attempts to "prove" Jesus' resurrection historically, to find analogous events of resuscitations and visions, to determine a historical cause for this event, are not only wrongheaded historically, they are wrongheaded theologically. Such approaches in the end actually soften the claim being made, cheapening its significance. No: Jesus of Nazareth was "raised from the dead on the third day," transformed to an immortal bodily existence untouched by sin and death, an event utterly unlike anything else in history, an event utterly uncaused by any human or historical process, a divine re-creation. To be sure, the Christian claim of Jesus' resurrection involves certain claims regarding effects of the resurrection as historical cause, events which can be examined historically. But determining a cause solely from its effects is a notoriously difficult endeavor, with a low probability of agreement regarding the results. And the nature of the resurrection makes this determination even more difficult: exactly what historical effects would one expect following an eschatological resurrection, a resurrection to a transformed creation? Once again we fail in finding a suitable analogy, and what remains is an ultimately improvable historical claim. A divine incursion from a temporal and spatial "other," summoning humanity to a re-created existence? Such is the scandal of the empty tomb.

In the end we are left not with historical arguments that lead to historical conclusions, nor with logical evidences that lead to logical conclusions. The basis for our belief in Jesus' resurrection stands—rather unnervingly for us—not within the safe boundaries of critical history but rather in the risky realm of faith: trusting in the primitive testimony of those very first witnesses as found in ancient traditions in later written records, and believing in the history-demanding yet history-defying claim that Jesus of Nazareth was "raised from the dead on the third day," transformed to an immortal bodily existence untouched by sin and death, a divine incursion into human history that itself transforms human history. Such is the scandal of the empty tomb, which, like the scandal of the cross, is a scandal which Christians should acknowledge, and even fully embrace.

To put this simply, everyone knows that dead people do not come back from the dead, let alone to some transformed human existence, but that's precisely the point of the Christian claim that God raised Jesus from the dead—the utterly impossible has in fact occurred. And the impossible has now become the norm, the standard by which all else is measured.

❧

Given the far-reaching implications of the vindication and renewal of humanity and creation brought about through the resurrection of Jesus, it is no surprise that Jesus' resurrection was at the very center of the gospel proclaimed by his earliest followers. Indeed, the entire Christian message of salvation is bound up in the cry "He is risen!" So Luke in Acts portrays the crucial criterion of apostleship as being "a witness of [Jesus'] resurrection" (Acts 1:22) and the early preaching of the apostles as "proclaiming in Jesus the resurrection of the dead" (Acts 4:2). As Paul put it, "if Christ has not been raised, your faith is futile; you are still in your sins" (1 Corinthians 15:17). This could perhaps be paraphrased this way: "If Christ has not been resurrected by God, Christian faith is pointless and salvation has not come to God's people—you might as well all go home and do something else!" However, to continue Paul's argument in the passage, "Christ has indeed been raised from the dead," and so a whole range of crucial, distinctively Christian beliefs and practices necessarily follow. In other words, the resurrection of the crucified Jesus is the ground and center of all truly Christian thought and action, both the source and the focus of all belief and behavior that can be called authentically Christian. The resurrection of the crucified Jesus was both the starting place and the compass for the first followers of Jesus in their journey to understand God and God's work in the world and to live out God's purposes for them, and so should it also be for Christians today.

Or, in other words, in the beginning God raised Jesus from the dead.

After reading . . .

- What two general ideas are involved in the concept of resurrection? In view of the biblical texts listed below, do you think this is an accurate or complete description of what "resurrection" means?

- What is involved in the biblical concept of "hope"? How is this different from or similar to the way the word "hope" is used in the world around you?

- What do you think of the idea that Jesus' resurrection cannot be proven through historical research? What is the basis for belief in Jesus' resurrection? How might this discussion affect your understanding of "faith" more generally?

- What does it mean to say that Jesus' resurrection is "the starting place and the compass" for all Christian theology? What do you think of this idea?

For further reading . . .

BIBLICAL TEXTS:
Psalm 16; Isaiah 26; Ezekiel 37; Daniel 12; Hosea 6; Matthew 28; John 20; Acts 1–4, 10, 13; Romans 8; 1 Corinthians 15; Philippians 3; 1 Thessalonians 4; Revelation 20.

Kirk, J. R. Daniel. *Unlocking Romans: Resurrection and the Justification of God.* Grand Rapids: Eerdmans, 2008.

A detailed, scholarly study of the way in which the concept of "resurrection" and the resurrection of Jesus is foundational to Paul's theology, particularly as expressed in Romans.

Longenecker, Richard N., ed. *Life in the Face of Death: The Resurrection Message of the New Testament.* Grand Rapids: Eerdmans, 1998.

A collection of essays that discusses the various perspectives on and dimensions of the concept of "resurrection" in earliest Christianity.

Madigan, Kevin J., and Jon D. Levenson. *Resurrection: The Power of God for Christians and Jews.* New Haven, Conn.: Yale University Press, 2008.

An accessible exploration of the origins of Jewish and Christian belief in "resurrection."

Williams, Rowan. *Resurrection: Interpreting the Easter Gospel.* 2nd ed. London: Darton, Longman & Todd, 2002.

A thoughtful description of how the theological significance of the resurrection of Jesus can be appropriated for Christian belief and practice today.

Wright, N. T. *The Resurrection of the Son of God.* Minneapolis: Fortress, 2003.

A thorough, scholarly study of the concept of "resurrection" and the resurrection of Jesus within the context of first-century AD Jewish and Greco-Roman thought.

———. *Surprised by Hope: Rethinking Heaven, the Resurrection, and the Mission of the Church.* New York: HarperOne, 2008.

A shorter, accessible treatment of the significance of the resurrection for Christian theology and practice, particularly in terms of eschatology and ecclesiology.

2

Crucifixion

Before you read . . .

- What comes to mind when you think of the word "sin"?
  How would you define "sin"?

- How would you describe the significance of Jesus' death
  on the cross? How does Jesus' death deal with sin?

JESUS' RESURRECTION SIMPLY cannot be established on standard critical historical grounds. Belief in this history-demanding yet history-defying event is an act of faith in the primitive testimony of early witnesses as reflected in ancient Christian traditions and writings. But Jesus' crucifixion is another matter. Jesus' death on a Roman cross outside Jerusalem is, according to the near-unanimity of historians, the most historically certain event in Jesus' life.

According to the canonical Gospels, the earliest extensive remembrances we have of Jesus' life and public career, Jesus knew his death was imminent. He told stories of his divine mission being like that of an envoy on behalf of a landowner, even the landowner's son, who goes to the landowner's estate to collect the profits on his investment—only to be killed by the servants in an act of greedy insurgence (Mark 12:1–11). He spoke of his life being like a single seed which is buried in the ground and dies for the sole purpose of bringing about new life (John 12:24). He even declared that his death was to have some sort of salvific significance, like a ransom for an enslaved prisoner or a confirmation of a new covenant (Mark 10:45; Luke 22:20). This sort of presentiment of death, even that one's death would have significance on behalf of others and that one would ultimately be vindicated through resurrection (Mark 8:31), was not unheard of in ancient Judaism. Indeed, one well-known story told of seven Jewish brothers who, in the face of execution, boldly proclaimed the significance of their impending deaths and the certainty of their vindicating resurrection (2 Maccabees 7).

But for Jesus this was more than simply a premonition of his execution. According to the Gospel remembrances, he seems even to have pushed circumstances so as virtually to guarantee his death during that final, fateful Passover in Jerusalem. During a festival attended by tens of thousands of Jewish pilgrims celebrating past deliverance from foreign oppression, the current "foreign oppressors," the Romans, were understandably nervous. Thus when Jesus entered Jerusalem on a donkey in deliberate fulfillment of an ancient prophecy regarding a future royal deliverer, with crowds crying out for just such a deliverance and waving palm branches as a national symbol of Jewish independence, the Romans undoubtedly took careful note of this latest messianic pretender (Mark 11:1–10). During one of the most important Jewish religious festivals, celebrating the initial event that led to the giving of the Law of Moses and the creation of the ancient people of

Israel, the Jewish religious leaders were understandably concerned that nothing disrupt their worship. Thus when Jesus
entered the Temple, the heart of both Jewish nationalism and
Israelite religion, and temporarily (and thus symbolically) disrupted the Temple worship, the Jewish religious leaders were
more than a little perturbed by this would-be prophet (Mark
11:15–18). And so, when Jesus challenged and defeated the
best debaters of the leading Jewish factions in public honor
contests in the Temple courts during that final week (Mark
11:27—12:40), his fate was sealed. Jesus had placed himself
irreversibly on the road to the cross.

$$\text{\reflectbox{Q}R}$$

As it impacts everything else at the heart of Christian faith,
Jesus' resurrection brings Jesus' death into sharper focus, im-
buing his crucifixion with enormous significance. Faced with
the mind-boggling reality that Jesus had been resurrected by
God, the earliest Christians had to make new sense of Jesus'
death. Because God raised Jesus from the dead, his death
could not merely be the oppressive and shameful crucifixion
of a wrongly condemned criminal. Jesus' death must also
have a divinely ordained significance, and this significance
was consistently understood by the New Testament authors
as related to dealing with sin. Though condemned under both
Jewish Torah and Roman law, Jesus was in fact righteous in
his relationship with God and innocent of the Roman charges
against him—a fact affirmed by God through his resurrection
of Jesus from the dead. Thus, his death was not for his own
sins but for the sins of others. Or, as it is worded in an early
gospel summary used by Paul and all the earliest apostles and
witnesses, Jesus died "for our sins" (1 Corinthians 15:3).

Sin is a multifaceted concept in the Christian Scriptures, and thus can be somewhat slippery to define. Many biblical writings describe specific "sins," behaviors or attitudes which are antithetical to God's will for humanity: pride, anger, slander, murder, selfishness, greed, lust, adultery, and more (e.g., Romans 1:28–31; Galatians 5:19–21). Many of these "sins" are depicted as specific acts of "unrighteousness" or "transgressions" of the Law of Moses which are committed by the Jewish people; yet Gentiles are not off the hook, and their sins are portrayed in terms of "ungodliness," "lawlessness," and the like. Some of the New Testament writings also refer to "sin" in the singular, as a sort of force or power that has corrupted or enslaved humanity and even all creation (e.g., John 8:34; Romans 3:9; 5:12–13; 7:14–23). In general, then, one can speak of "sin" producing "sins"—the power of "sin" which holds sway over humanity works itself out in the specific "sins" of individual persons, those attitudes and behaviors which work against God's purposes for humanity as created in God's image.

These biblical notions of sin have their roots in one of the first stories of Genesis (Genesis 2–3). In this story the original creation is depicted as a garden filled with goodness and beauty in which human beings dwell in harmony with God and nature. But this pristine creation is disrupted and corrupted when the first humans disobey God's command and feel the full effects of their sin. Shame in relationships (3:7, 10), guilt in trespassing a divine command (3:11), hostility within creation (3:15), physical pain and suffering (3:16–17), systemic human oppression (3:16), a sense of futility in life and work (3:17–19), physical death (3:19), exclusion from life as God intended it (3:22–24)—all these realities are summed up by a comprehensive concept of "death" as the result of sin (see 2:17). Thus the power of "sin" works itself out in specific "sins," all of which bring about a wide-ranging "death" that permeates the human condition within creation.

While the reality of sin was assumed by the earliest Christians, it was confirmed by the death of Jesus. For the resurrected Jesus to have been crucified "for our sins" means that human sin must be a serious matter indeed, even the ultimate problem faced by humanity, systemic and incurable. Yet both this general "sin" and these specific "sins" are decisively dealt with by the death of Jesus. The New Testament writings uniformly affirm this, but there are a variety of specific ways in which they describe this, using an assortment of metaphors and stories derived from the Jewish Scriptures.

The first idea that features in some prominent texts is that *Jesus was the perfect sin offering in atonement for the guilt and estrangement of sin.* This notion draws on the system of animal sacrifices used among the ancient Israelites and codified in the Law of Moses. The regular guilt and sin offerings made "atonement" for the sins of the person who offered them; that is, God viewed them as in some sense making amends for the specific transgressions of the Law committed by that person, making possible divine pardon of those transgressions. This was because, as the priestly code of Moses explained, "the life of a creature is in the blood, and . . . it is the blood that makes atonement for one's life" (Leviticus 17:11). Sin brings death—as every Israelite already knew from the stories found in the first chapters of Genesis—and a life must be given in exchange for one's life. The annual Day of Atonement highlighted this reality even further: the double goats represented twin results of sinning against God—death and exclusion—and so in order to secure Israel's continued covenant life and relationship with God, one goat must be killed, while the other must be expelled (Leviticus 16).

This image of sacrificial atonement captures one essential aspect of the significance of Jesus' death "for our sins." As Paul puts it in his letter to the Romans, "God presented Christ as a sacrifice of atonement, through the shedding of his blood" (Romans 3:25). Or, in the words of 1 John, Jesus is "the atoning sacrifice for our sins, and not only for ours but also for the sins of the whole world" (1 John 2:2). The blood sacrifice of Jesus on a Roman cross makes amends for human sin and makes possible divine pardon of those sins. In his sacrificial death Jesus gave his life for our life; in his death outside the gates of Jerusalem Jesus was excluded so that we could be fully embraced by God.

A second New Testament concept for interpreting Jesus' death was that *Jesus was the unblemished Passover lamb in redemption from the slavery and oppression of sin.* This image conjures up not a law code but a story, the story of God's deliverance of the people of Israel from slavery in Egypt. As the story of Jesus would become the foundational narrative of Christianity, decisively shaping its convictions and values, so the story of the exodus was the foundational narrative of the Jewish people. In this great event described in the book of Exodus, God had redeemed the people of Israel, buying them back from slavery and delivering them into freedom. Through the exodus God had guided and provided for the people of Israel, showing his great power in protecting them from Egypt's mighty armies and showing his great love in caring for them in the hostile desert. At the center of this process God had created the people of Israel as a distinct nation, establishing a formal agreement or covenant built around mutual love and faithfulness as expressed in the Law given through Moses (Exodus 19–24). And all this was made possible through the blood of an unblemished lamb (Exodus 12).

Of course this image of a Passover lamb was a natural one for the New Testament authors to use, given that Jesus was crucified at the time of Passover as the Jewish people gathered in Jerusalem to celebrate God's salvation and formation of his people. Thus Jesus' death is described in John's Gospel as occurring right at the time when the Passover lambs were slaughtered (John 19:14), and the language of "redemption" from the enslavement of sin permeates the New Testament writings in describing the meaning of Jesus' death. As Paul says plainly, "Christ, our Passover lamb, has been sacrificed" (1 Corinthians 5:7), and this has great significance for the faith and life of the followers of Jesus, now set free from the power of sin.

A third interpretive image is found among the New Testament writings related to Jesus' death: *Jesus was the sacrifice required to ratify a new-covenant relationship apart from sin.* This image also recalled the exodus and the covenant God made through Moses, but viewed these through the lens of a later story in ancient Israel's history: the exile and prophetic promises of a new covenant for God's people. As God had warned would happen in the initial covenant through Moses, the people of Israel were eventually scattered among the nations after their systemic failure to keep his Law. First the northern tribes and then the southern tribes were conquered by the world powers of their day, Assyria and then Babylonia, and Israel was banished from her promised land. In the midst of this catastrophic upheaval, prophets rose up to warn the people of this coming divine discipline and to comfort the people with promises of God's future restoration, a restoration which would include a new covenant. As the prophet Jeremiah proclaimed on God's behalf, "'The days are coming,' declares the Lord, 'when I will make a new covenant with the house of Israel and with the house of Judah. . . . I will put my Law in their minds and write it on their hearts. I will be their God, and they will be my people. . . . I will forgive their wickedness and will remember their sins no more'" (Jeremiah 31:31–34).

This image of a new covenant bringing the full restoration of God's people with the full forgiveness of their sins is taken up by the New Testament authors and applied to Jesus' death. Just as the covenant through Moses was only ratified through a blood sacrifice (Exodus 24), so the new covenant would require the shedding of blood to be put into effect. Thus both Luke and Paul describe Jesus' words at the Last Supper with his disciples before his death, "This cup is the new covenant in my blood" (Luke 22:20; 1 Corinthians 11:25)—in other words, Jesus' death was to bring about the promised new covenant, and the cup of wine represents his blood by which this new covenant is ratified. The author of Hebrews sums it up nicely: "Christ is the mediator of a new covenant" (Hebrews 9:15), establishing an eternal new relationship of deep intimacy between God and his people through Jesus' sacrificial death on a cross.

Another image was also used by the earliest Christians to make sense of Jesus' crucifixion: *Jesus was the ideal example of one who gave his life in the cause of good and righteousness over evil and sin.* Like other groups around them, the Jews of Jesus' day had their own stories of martyrs for their cause.

The seven brothers mentioned earlier fit into this category, martyrs in the face of foreign pressure to paganism, standing up for Jewish ethnic and religious distinctiveness as divinely prescribed by the Torah. Other, more ancient heroes were also readily available to be emulated: Daniel and his three friends risking their lives in standing up for Jewish obedience to Torah (Daniel 1–6); young David's death-defying stand against the evil Goliath and the Philistine hordes (1 Samuel 17); even Abel's death at the hands of Cain simply because he offered his sacrifices in a manner which pleased God (Genesis 4). David was especially significant in this, as the many "psalms of David" frequently attest to his loyal dependence on God in the midst of unjust suffering at the hands of evil men. All these and more provided important examples for the Jewish people of faithfulness to God and God's good purposes in spite of unjust suffering and pressure to be unfaithful.

For the earliest Christians, Jesus' suffering and death were viewed in this same way. As Jesus was the "son of David," his messianic descendent, it was natural to look to David's psalms to make sense of Jesus' unjust suffering at the hands of evil men. So Psalm 22, for example, provided a crucial framework for the Gospel authors in describing Jesus' suffering on the cross (e.g., Mark 15:34). And just as Jesus took up his cross, denying himself in his own desires and needs, so also his followers must deny themselves, take up their own crosses, and follow him (Mark 8:34). Or, as 1 Peter affirms, "Christ suffered for you, leaving you an example, that you should follow in his steps" (1 Peter 2:21). The author of Hebrews echoes this idea, affirming that we should be "fixing our eyes on Jesus, the pioneer and perfecter of faith. For the joy set before him he endured the cross, scorning its shame, and sat down at the right hand of the throne of God. Consider him who endured such opposition from sinners, so that you will not grow weary and lose heart" (Hebrews 12:2–3). Paul paints this image in a very personal way: "I have been crucified with Christ and I no longer live, but Christ lives in me. The life I now live in the body, I live by faith in the Son of God, who loved me and gave himself for me" (Galatians 2:20). Jesus' death provides a cross-shaped pattern for Christians to follow in their own struggle against sin both within themselves and in the world.

One final image is also evident in the New Testament writings to interpret Jesus' death: *Jesus was the paradoxical victor who submitted to sin's darkest weapon and thus defeated the sinister forces of this present age.* This motif comes from some of the darker, more difficult stories of Judaism, the cosmic stories of an apocalyptic worldview. In this Jewish apocalypticism, human life in the visible world was thought to be like a play on a stage—behind the actions of those in the play lie unseen forces which exert their control over the actors, even a pre-determined script which moves the actors inexorably toward the play's conclusion. These unseen forces could be personal spiritual forces such as a devil and the demonic, or socio-political or socio-economic forces such as kings and empires, or even more impersonal anthropological forces such as sin and death—the darkest of the bunch. This sort of apocalyptic perspective can be seen, for example, in the book of Daniel, with its description of angelic powers in a cosmic struggle of good versus evil, and its visions of the inevitable rise and fall of earthly kingdoms ultimately crushed by God's own kingdom (Daniel 7–12).

For the New Testament authors Jesus had tackled these powers of the present age head on, ultimately taking on death, sin's most menacing weapon, and had come through victorious and triumphant. Ironically, by submitting to these evil powers and surrendering to death, Jesus defeated them. In the words of Jesus in John's Gospel, speaking of his upcoming death, "now the prince of this world"—the devil himself—"will be driven out" (John 12:31). Or as Paul affirms in his letter to the Colossians, "having disarmed the powers and authorities, [Jesus] made a public spectacle of them, triumphing over them by the cross" (Colossians 2:15). In his crucifixion Jesus conquered the unjust conquerors of this age—including even the otherwise unstoppable twin powers of sin and death.

While Christians have often emphasized one or two of these interpretations of Jesus' death over others, creating de-tailed "atonement theories," all of these logically distinct yet theologically connected ideas were represented in the diverse thought of the earliest Christians. Jesus' death was viewed as an atoning sacrifice, reversing the guilt and estrangement of sin; it was interpreted as a Passover sacrifice, bringing redemption and liberation from sin's enslavement; his death was understood as a covenant-ratification sacrifice, establish-ing a new relationship between God and his people; it was seen as an example to follow in standing up to the sin and evil of the world through suffering; and it was regarded as a paradoxical victory over the evil forces of this present age. All five of these interpretive images are necessary for delving into the deep significance of Jesus' salvific death as dealing with the full range of sin's effects, providing a kaleidoscope of perspectives on the resurrection-inspired meaning of Jesus' crucifixion.

CR

A single dominant thread is woven through this fabric of diverse interpretations of Jesus' death "for our sins": Jesus' self-giving on behalf of others, even those who would seem least to deserve it. This should not be surprising in light of the early Christian stories of Jesus' life and teaching found in the Gospels.

Such complete self-giving for the benefit of others, even for those viewed by the world as the last, the least, and the lost, was summed up by Jesus and his first followers in a single, simple yet profound word: *love*. Jesus described God's entire will for humanity, the Great Commandment, with this one powerful word, expanding the foundational Jewish creed, the *Shema*, to enfold the love of others within one's love for God: "'Love the Lord your God with all your heart and with all your soul and with all your mind.' This is the first and greatest commandment. And the second is like it: 'Love your neighbor as yourself'" (Matthew 22:37–40; see Deuteronomy 6:4–5; Leviticus 19:18). And Jesus' actions lined up with his words. One of his characteristic activities was his full table fellowship with "sinners," those on the fringes of acceptable Jewish society, even some who were considered beyond the pale. He welcomed to his table those who were despised, even anticipating through this action God's future welcome of the sinful and the oppressed and the marginalized into the kingdom of God, the eternal sovereign and saving reign of God over creation.

Jesus' self-giving death for the benefit of sinful humanity was thus the final, definitive demonstration of a whole life of love, a divine revelation of love stamped with God's seal of approval by God's resurrection of the crucified Jesus from the dead.

After reading . . .

- What does it mean to say that "'sin' produces 'sins'"? How do you see this kind of "sin" or "sins" in your own life, or in the world around you?

- What are the five biblical images used in the New Testament to explain Jesus' death "for sins"? Which of these five do you find the most helpful in understanding Jesus' death for your sins? In view of the biblical texts listed below, do you think these five images together provide an accurate or complete description of the significance of Jesus' death on the cross?

- How is the "love" taught by Jesus and demonstrated by him in his life and death different from other conceptions of "love" in the world around you? How is it similar? How might you live out Jesus' love in your world?

For further reading . . .

BIBLICAL TEXTS:
Exodus 12; Leviticus 16–17; Psalm 22; Isaiah 53; Jeremiah 31; Mark 8, 11–12, 15; John 15, 19; Romans 3; 1 Corinthians 13; Colossians 2; Hebrews 8–10; 1 Peter 2–3; 1 John 3–4.

Carroll, John T., and Joel B. Green. *The Death of Jesus in Early Christianity.* Peabody, MA: Hendrickson, 1995.

A collection of essays that explores the various perspectives on and interpretations of the death of Jesus within earliest Christianity.

Gorman, Michael J. *Cruciformity: Paul's Narrative Spirituality of the Cross.* Grand Rapids: Eerdmans, 2001.

An exploration of Paul's distinctive emphasis on Jesus' self-giving, life-giving death as a pattern for Christian life, ministry, and ethics.

Green, Joel B., and Mark D. Baker. *Recovering the Scandal of the Cross: Atonement in New Testament and Contemporary Contexts.* Downers Grove, IL: InterVarsity, 2000.

A discussion of the various images used to understand Jesus' death in the New Testament and throughout Christian history.

Hengel, Martin. *Crucifixion in the Ancient World and the Folly of the Message of the Cross.* Philadelphia: Fortress, 1977.

A study of the practice and significance of crucifixion in the ancient world and the place of Jesus' crucifixion within that ancient setting.

Jervis, L. Ann. *At the Heart of the Gospel: Suffering in the Earliest Christian Message.* Grand Rapids: Eerdmans, 2007.

An exploration of the significance of suffering in the thought of the New Testament authors, particularly how the suffering of Jesus relates to the suffering of his followers.

McKnight, Scot. *The Jesus Creed: Loving God, Loving Others.* Brewster, MA: Paraclete, 2004.

An accessible treatment of the Great Commandment of Jesus and its implications for Christian spirituality and ethics.

———. *Jesus and His Death: Historiography, the Historical Jesus, and Atonement Theory.* Waco, TX: Baylor University Press, 2005.

A thorough, scholarly discussion of the question of how Jesus viewed his own death, especially as related to the historic atonement theories of Christianity.

———. *A Community Called Atonement.* Living Theology. Nashville, TN: Abingdon, 2007.

An accessible exploration of the meaning of Jesus' death as "atonement" and the significance of this for Christians and Christian communities today.

3

Son

Before you read . . .

- Can you think of some portrayals of Jesus in movies, or books, or paintings, or songs? What do these emphasize about Jesus? Why do you think Jesus has so captured the imagination of authors, artists, musicians, and film-makers throughout history, even those who are not Christians?

- How would you describe the significance of Jesus in terms of his identity, or who he is?

FOR THE EARLIEST Christians, the resurrection of the crucified Jesus inevitably prompted not only a new way of thinking about his death but also a new way of thinking about Jesus himself. His resurrection by God signaled that not only his death but also his whole life and career—indeed, Jesus' very identity and personhood—had divine significance, that Jesus was in fact the focal point of God's activity in human history.

There are several ways of getting at this early Christian understanding of Jesus' identity and personhood, but perhaps the easiest way is to explore the three most common titles used by the New Testament authors to describe Jesus, three titles which point to three distinct yet vitally connected stories.

ભ

One of the earliest Christian confessions of faith was that Jesus is the "Christ" (from Greek) or "Messiah" (from Hebrew), the "Anointed One." To tell the story of the "Messiah" one must begin at least as far back as the biblical narratives of King David; to tell the story *well* demands that one reach all the way back to the Genesis creation stories.

According to these sacred stories, humanity was created in "the image of God" (Genesis 1:26–27). As these early chapters of Genesis unfold, this concept of *imago Dei* is spelled out in two related metaphors: God as king, and God as father. The creation narrative describes God's human-creating command this way: "Let us make human beings *in our image, in our likeness, so that they may rule* over the fish in the sea and the birds in the sky, over the livestock and all the wild animals, and over all the creatures that move along the ground" (Genesis 1:26, emphasis added). The idea that God is King over his creation means that human beings created in "the image of God" function as his vassal kings, his royal representatives extending and ensuring God's loving and faithful rule over the earth. As for the second metaphor, the idea that God is Father of humanity means that human beings created in "the image of God" have a relationship with God which is unique among created beings, that in some sense human beings share God's distinctive features as a child reflects the likeness of his or her parents. That this is an element of the language of "image" or "likeness" can be seen in the primal genealogy of Genesis: "When God created human beings, he made them *in the likeness of God*. He created them male and female and blessed them. . . . When Adam had lived 130 years, he had a son *in his own likeness, in his own image*" (Genesis 5:1–3). The convergence of these two metaphors in the concept of the "image of God" suggests that God's kingdom—his sovereign, sustaining rule over his creation—was to be mediated on earth by humanity, God's unique representatives in a unique relationship with him, uniquely reflecting God's character.

However, the story immediately takes a dark turn when humanity fails in this relationship and responsibility (Genesis 3). In response God chooses a people, the descendants of Abraham, Isaac, and Jacob, the people of Israel, to be a "blessing" to "all peoples on earth" (Genesis 12:2–3), to be a "kingdom of priests" on behalf of humanity (Exodus 19:5–6), collectively to be God's "son" embodying the character of God (Exodus 4:22–23).

These twin themes of "kingship" and "sonship" meet again in a unique promise God makes to David, ancient Israel's greatest king. According to the biblical narrative, David has conquered his enemies and established his kingdom in Israel. After building a palace (a "house") for himself, he decides it is time to build a "house" (a temple) for God. God responds to David with a promise: David is not to build a "house" for God, but God will in fact build a "house" (a dynasty) for David. As God declares to David, "I will raise up your offspring to succeed you, one of your own sons, and I will establish his kingdom. . . . I will be his father, and he will be my son. . . . I will set him over my house and my kingdom forever; his throne will be established forever" (1 Chronicles 17:10–14). Thus, each of the kings in the family line of David would rule as "king" and "son," even ruling over God's own kingdom as part of God's own dynasty.

This Davidic promise formed the basis of most "messianic" expectations among the Jewish people through to Jesus' day. Many believed that a "Messiah"—suggesting one who is "anointed" as a king—would one day rise up and truly fulfill this promise; one in the line of David would establish God's kingdom on earth forever, re-instating God's sovereign, sustaining, and salvific reign throughout the earth. This expectation is especially evident in the biblical writings among the Old Testament prophets. Isaiah, Jeremiah, Ezekiel, and others anticipated a coming descendant of David, both a king and a son, who would bring about God's kingdom on earth, even bringing creation back to its original Edenic bliss and blessing (e.g., Isaiah 9:6–7; 11:1–9; Jeremiah 33:14–26; Ezekiel 34:11–31).

For the early Christians the story of the "Messiah" found its conclusion in the story of Jesus. The Gospels describe Jesus' teaching as characteristically concerned with the "kingdom of God," the eschatological sovereign and saving rule of God over creation. While the Gospels never portray Jesus as using the title "Christ" or "Messiah" for himself, they certainly reflect the memory of Jesus' acceptance of that title by others and his fulfillment of messianic expectations through his actions. So Peter confessed to Jesus, "You are the Messiah" (Mark 8:29), and when Jesus was asked by John the Baptist's followers if he were "the one who was to come" (Luke 7:20), Jesus answered by pointing to his merciful and miraculous actions as indications that the kingdom of God promised by Isaiah was finally being established (Luke 7:21–22; Isaiah 61:1).

However, while Jesus acknowledged this title, he was in many ways not the Messiah people anticipated, and the "kingdom of God" he brought about was not the kingdom most people expected. Nowhere is this more evident than in the account common to the first three Gospels outlining Peter's confession and Jesus' subsequent teaching (Mark 8:27–35). Since Jesus accepted the title of "Messiah" from Peter's lips, one might have expected him to describe his mission as going to Jerusalem, raising an army of insurgents along the way, in order to overthrow the Roman oppressors and establish the kingdom as it was during the glory days of David. Instead, Jesus was remembered as interpreting the title and its necessary task in very different, even opposite, terms: he is going to Jerusalem to die on a Roman cross at the hands of his enemies, expecting to be vindicated by God through resurrection. Unlike the kingdoms and empires of human history, the kingdom of God is a kingdom ruled by an utterly self-giving, beneficent king. John's Gospel certainly has it right in Jesus' declaration before the Roman governor Pontius Pilate: "My kingdom is not of this world" (John 18:36). In other words, God's kingdom does not originate in this dark and dying world, and it is not like this world's kingdoms.

Jesus' crucifixion, then, did not spell the end of God's kingdom on earth; in fact, in a very real sense his suffering and death enacted the kingdom of God, demonstrating its central character and enabling it to come to fruition. Moreover, by resurrecting the crucified Jesus from the dead, God put a divine seal of approval on Jesus' title and his task, as the Messiah establishing the kingdom of God on earth. In the life, death, and resurrection of Jesus, the saving, sovereign rule of

God over creation has arrived. The promise of *imago Dei* has finally been fulfilled.

CR

A second very primitive Christian confession of faith was that Jesus is "Lord." This title also points to a story, a story told in answer to two questions, "Whose world is this?" and "Whose people are we?"

This story in many ways parallels the story of "Messiah," and it also begins back in the creation beliefs of ancient Israel. A strong motif running through the Jewish Scriptures is that there is only one God, creation's Creator, and that this God is the God of Israel. As Creator, God owns the patent on all creation; the world is his world, and all that is in it finds its purpose in his purpose. As the biblical narrative unfolds, this Creator God reveals himself to Moses and the people of Israel as *YHWH* (*Yahweh*). Out of reverence for this divine name, the people of Israel began to substitute the title *Adonai* in its place, which is translated into Greek as *Kyrios* and into English as "Lord." Thus, the Jewish answer to the question "Whose world is this?" has always been "The world belongs to *YHWH*, the only Creator, the God of Israel, and the only all-sovereign Lord."

According to the account in Exodus 3, God revealed this divine name to Moses at a crucial point in Israel's history. The descendants of Israel were enslaved in Egypt, crying out to God for deliverance. Moses was raised up as God's appointed deliverer for Israel, providentially prepared for his mission, and it was at the moment of Moses' commission before the burning bush that God declared the divine name to him:

YHWH. It was a covenant name, a name which solidified the relationship between God and his people, a name whose meaning for the ancient Israelites could well be paraphrased as "I always have been, always am, and always will be everything you need me to be." And so *YHWH* was indeed "everything his people needed him to be," redeeming them from slavery in Egypt, establishing them as his people in their own land. Thus, the Jewish answer to the question "Whose people are we?" has always been "We belong to *YHWH*, the only Creator, the God of Israel, and the only all-sovereign Lord."

But other people gave very different answers to these questions. Over the centuries, other "gods" and "lords" were affirmed among the nations, and these "gods" and "lords" competed with Israel's God for the sovereign rights to the world and its people. By the time of Jesus, there were dozens of different political, religious, and philosophical answers to the questions, "Whose world is this?" and "Whose people are we?" Perhaps the most prominent of these—certainly the one most able to be backed up with concrete evidence—was the answer given by Rome: "The world and its people belong to Rome and her Emperor, the only all-sovereign Lord."

For the earliest Christians, the conclusion to this story and the answers to these questions were declared by God in his resurrection of the crucified Jesus. Psalm 110 was highly significant in shaping this early Christian understanding of Jesus. This psalm, a "psalm of David" and likely viewed among ancient Jews as a description of the coming messianic descendant of David, opens with these words: "The Lord (*YHWH*) says to my Lord (*Adonai*): 'Sit at my right hand until I make your enemies a footstool for your feet.' The Lord (*YHWH*) will extend your mighty scepter from Zion, saying,

'Rule in the midst of your enemies'" (Psalm 110:1–2). The Old Greek translation commonly used by the Greek-speaking early Christians, the Septuagint, uses the word *Kyrios* for both *YHWH* and *Adonai*. And so this messianic psalm was taken as a description of Jesus and the word *Kyrios* or "Lord" as a title for Jesus in light of his resurrection from the dead. God had resurrected the crucified Jesus from the dead, vindicating him as the Christ, and had exalted the resurrected Jesus to his "right hand," acknowledging Jesus' full authority as Lord. As Peter's Pentecost sermon in Acts concludes, through Jesus' resurrection and exaltation "God has made this Jesus, whom you crucified, both Lord and Messiah" (Acts 2:36). Thus, the Christian answer to the question "Whose world is this?" is a resounding declaration: "The world belongs to *YHWH*, the only Creator God, through Jesus, the only all-sovereign Lord."

Just as the term "Lord" brought the themes of relationship and redemption to mind for the ancient Israelites, so it was for the earliest Christians. It is because Jesus is Lord that Jesus can also be Savior; it is because Jesus is sovereign over all God's creation and victorious over all God's cosmic enemies that he can deliver God's people from the slavery of their sin and the oppression of evil in this world. Thus, the Christian answer to the question "Whose people are we?" is the same resounding declaration: "We belong to *YHWH*, the only Creator God, through Jesus, the only all-sovereign Lord." Or, as Paul phrases this answer, "for us there is but one God, the Father, from whom all things came and for whom we live; and there is but one Lord, Jesus Christ, through whom all things came and through whom we live" (1 Corinthians 8:6).

෬

A third early Christian title for Jesus deserves mention here, that of Jesus as "Son of God." Again, a story lies in the background of this title, a story which in its earlier parts directly parallels the story of the "Messiah."

We have already noted the twin themes of "kingship" and "sonship" in reference to the concept of "Messiah." Humanity was created in the "image of God," to be as God's vassal kings mediating God's rule over the earth, and to be as God's children reflecting God's character. The dynastic kings in the line of David were to fulfill these twin roles of being "God's king" and "God's son." Thus the title "Son of God" originated as a royal title, not a title of divinity. It was a designation for the very human kings in the family line of David, and it thus became a designation of the expected Messiah, also very much thought of by most expectant Jews as a human being.

The story of the "Son of God" continued to parallel that of the "Messiah" right through the earliest applications of this title to Jesus. In fact, it is likely that we should read "Son of God" simply as equivalent to "Messiah" or "Christ" in many of its uses in the New Testament writings. So Peter's confession of Jesus as Messiah in Mark's Gospel ("You are the Christ"; Mark 8:29) gets expanded with the equivalent "Son of God" in Matthew's Gospel ("You are the Christ, the Son of the living God"; Matthew 16:16). Similar equivalences between "Christ" and "Son of God" are evident at least in the first three Gospels and perhaps beyond, and we should be careful not to read more into these texts than is warranted: Jesus is being described as the promised human descendant of David who would bring about God's kingdom on earth.

However, in the light of the resurrection of Jesus, the title "Son of God" took on added significance. Jesus was remembered by the earliest Christians as having referred to God as *Abba* (Mark 14:36). This was an Aramaic word with some similarities to the English "Papa" or "Dad," bringing to mind both the providential care and the unquestioned authority expected of good fathers in Jesus' day while also connoting a strong sense of personal intimacy. While similar "Father" language was often used of God in relationship with Israel collectively as his "children," it would have been somewhat unusual for an individual Jewish man to speak of God in such personal terms, as his *Abba*. This lingering memory of Jesus' characteristic speech among the early Christians points to Jesus having seen his relationship with God as distinctive. The combination of this intimate use of *Abba* for God with other remembrances of Jesus, such as his strong sense of divine purpose expressed in several "I have come…" sayings (e.g., Matthew 10:34–35), moved the early Christians to see Jesus' relationship with God as more than distinctive, even as unique.

It was natural, then, that this idea of Jesus' unique relationship as a Son with God as his Father would become signified by the messianic title "Son of God." This expanded understanding of Jesus' "Sonship" can be seen to some extent in Paul's writings and then especially in the writings of John. While the title "Son of God" continues to carry the equivalence of "Messiah" even in these writings, it takes on additional weight. So Paul states in Romans that the gospel is about "[God's] Son, who as to his earthly life was a descendant of David, and who through the Spirit of holiness was appointed the Son of God in power by his resurrection from the dead: Jesus Christ our Lord" (Romans 1:3–4). Jesus as "Son of God" is the promised descendant of David, that is, the Messiah; and by raising Jesus from the dead God appointed him as, even more, the "Son of God in power." In a similar way John's Gospel was written to create and sustain the belief "that Jesus is the Messiah, the Son of God" (John 20:31), while at the same time highlighting the fact that the resurrected Jesus is worthy even to be called "Lord and God" (John 20:28). As the "Son of God," Jesus is the promised Messiah; but as the "Son of God," Jesus is more than simply a human Messiah. He is, to use one of John's distinctive phrases, the "one and only Son of God," united with God the Father in purpose, in relationship, and even in identity.

This exalted view of Jesus is also reflected in other ways in the New Testament. For at least some of the earliest Christians, Jesus' identification with God meant that the characteristic actions of God—the divine actions of creation and salvation, for instance—were also ascribed to Jesus. Using the language of the Jewish wisdom tradition which personified "wisdom" as the instrument of God's creation (e.g., Proverbs 8:22–31), Jesus is described as the agent of God's creation in several New Testament texts: he is the "Son . . . through [whom God] made the universe" (Hebrews 1:2); "in him all things were created: things in heaven and on earth, visible and invisible, whether thrones or powers or rulers or authorities; all things have been created through him and for him" (Colossians 1:16); and "through him all things were made; without him nothing was made that has been made" (John 1:3). Likewise the language of "Savior"—reserved in the Jewish Scriptures for God—is applied in the New Testament at least as often to the crucified and resurrected Jesus: he is exalted to God's right hand as "Prince and Savior" of Israel (Acts 5:31); he is even the "Savior of the world" (John 4:42; 1 John 4:14), the Savior "who has destroyed death and has brought life and immortality to light through the gospel" (2 Timothy 1:10).

೮౩

The resurrection of the crucified Jesus thus necessitated a new way of thinking about Jesus for the earliest Christians, even to the extent of understanding Jesus' identity as having been caught up into the very identity of God. The stories behind the titles "Messiah," "Lord," and "Son of God" were very much stories about God, yet for the first Christians Jesus became the hero in these stories, fulfilling God's purposes, doing God's actions, displaying God's character—uniquely embodying *YHWH*, the Creator God, the Divine King, the Sovereign Lord, the Loving Father.

The resurrection of the crucified Jesus necessitates a new way of thinking about Jesus, but the resurrection of Jesus in itself does not demonstrate that Jesus was Messiah, or Lord, or Son of God. After all, Christians can expect to be resurrected just like Jesus, yet that will not make any individual Christian into the unique Messiah, Lord, or Son of God. Rather, the resurrection functioned much like a divine stamp of approval, indicating that the stories of "Messiah," "Lord," and "Son of God" which had been taken up by Jesus and the earliest Christians in reference to him were in fact valid narratives for understanding Jesus. Jesus was the satisfactory conclusion to these stories, and his resurrection was God's imprimatur, the divine declaration that the story of Jesus—the "good news"—was ready to be published to the world.

After reading . . .

- What does it mean to affirm that Jesus is "Messiah" or "Christ"? that he is "Lord"? that he is "Son of God"? Which of these titles do you find most helpful to you in your understanding of Jesus?

- What does it mean to say that Jesus "uniquely embodies" God? What does this tell us about Jesus? What does this tell us about God?

For further reading . . .

BIBLICAL TEXTS:

Genesis 1; Exodus 3; 1 Chronicles 17; Psalm 110; Isaiah 9; 11; Daniel 7; Mark 8; John 1, 20; Acts 2; Romans 1; 1 Corinthians 8; Philippians 2; Colossians 1; Hebrews 1–2; Revelation 1.

Bauckham, Richard. *Jesus and the God of Israel: God Crucified and Other Studies on the New Testament's Christology of Divine Identity.* Grand Rapids: Eerdmans, 2008.

A detailed exploration of the early Christian understanding of the divine identity of Jesus, particularly in light of Jesus' life, death, and resurrection.

Bird, Michael F. *Are You the One Who Is to Come? The Historical Jesus and the Messianic Question.* Grand Rapids: Baker, 2009.

A study of Jesus' identity as Messiah, especially Jesus' own understanding of this as expressed through his distinctive actions and sayings.

Dunn, James D. G. *Jesus Remembered.* Grand Rapids: Eerdmans, 2003.

A thorough, scholarly study of the life and teaching of Jesus, including his own understanding of his identity.

Fee, Gordon D. *Pauline Christology: An Exegetical-Theological Study.* Peabody, MA: Hendrickson, 2007.

A detailed study of the passages in Paul's letters that speak of the identity and significance of Jesus.

Hurtado, Larry W. *How on Earth Did Jesus Become a God? Historical Questions about Earliest Devotion to Jesus.* Grand Rapids: Eerdmans, 2005.

An accessible treatment of the development of early Christian thinking about Jesus' divine identity.

————. *Lord Jesus Christ: Devotion to Jesus in Earliest Christianity.* Grand Rapids: Eerdmans, 2003.

A more thorough, scholarly study of the development of early Christian thinking about Jesus' divine identity.

Neufeld, Thomas R. Yoder. *Recovering Jesus: The Witness of the New Testament.* Grand Rapids: Brazos, 2007.

An introduction to the life, teaching, and identity of Jesus as reflected in the New Testament.

Pannenberg, Wolfhart. *Jesus: God and Man.* 2nd ed. Philadelphia: Westminster, 1977.

A scholarly exploration of the Christian doctrine of Christology, including Jesus' divine-human identity and the theological significance of his life, death, and especially resurrection.

Wright, N. T. *The Challenge of Jesus: Rediscovering Who Jesus Was and Is.* Downers Grove, IL: InterVarsity, 1999.

An accessible treatment of the life, teaching, and identity of Jesus.

————. *Jesus and the Victory of God.* Minneapolis: Fortress, 1996.

A more thorough, scholarly study of the life and teaching of Jesus, including his own understanding of his identity.

4

Gospel

Before you read . . .

- Can you think of any popular summaries of the gospel used in Christian evangelism? What are the key elements of the gospel in these summaries?

- How would you summarize the gospel?

So FAR OUR attempt to re-trace the theological journey of the first Christians has brought us to a fuller understanding of Jesus, his death, and his resurrection. Now we must bring these three vistas together into a full panorama of the most essential Christian beliefs. These three elements are consistently found at the heart of New Testament descriptions of the "gospel," the Christian "good news" of salvation. Whether one examines the central motifs of the Gospels (e.g., Mark 8:31), the evangelistic speeches in Acts (e.g., 2:23–24), the summaries of belief or gospel in Paul's letters (e.g., Romans 1:1–4; 4:24–25), or the salvation descriptions in the later New Testament (e.g., 1 Peter 1:18–21), one finds the crucified and resurrected Jesus to be the core of the Christian message of salvation.

This is clearly evident in what is perhaps the most important passage in the Christian Scriptures, another of Paul's gospel summaries:

> I want to remind you of the gospel I preached to you, which you received and on which you have taken your stand. By this gospel you are saved . . . For what I received I passed on to you as of first importance:
>
> that Christ died for our sins according to the Scriptures,
> that he was buried,
> that he was raised on the third day according to the Scriptures,
> and that he appeared to Peter, and then to the Twelve. . . .
>
> Whether, then, it is I or they, this is what we preach, and this is what you believed.
> (1 Corinthians 15:1–11)

In this passage Paul uses somewhat technical language from the ancient world for the transmission of oral traditions ("received . . . passed on") to highlight the statement as well-established teaching which Paul learned from someone else. Paul may even have received this "gospel creed" from Peter or another apostle within a few years of Jesus, which would make this statement the earliest witness to the Christian gospel we possess. Moreover, this gospel message focused on Jesus Christ, his death "for our sins," and his resurrection "on the third day," all "according to the Scriptures," is described as the most foundational and unifying element of Christian faith. It is "of first importance," and it is through persevering faith in this message that salvation is brought about. And in his concluding statement Paul indicates that this traditional, essential gospel message is that which was consistently preached by all the eyewitnesses and apostles of the resurrected Jesus. For the earliest Christians, the gospel of salvation was all about Jesus, his death, and his resurrection.

We have already explored each of these three elements in the previous three chapters. However, before we can bring these thoughts together into a coherent description of the gospel, there are two other ancient "gospels" which need to be explored in order to provide some further context.

⍟

The first of these is the "gospel" according to the prophet Isaiah. For the earliest Christians, all devout Jews, the language of "good news" had particular connotations arising from the Jewish Scriptures, with the second half of the book of Isaiah (Isaiah 40–66) providing a crucial lens through which the rest of the Scriptures were read.

This portion of Isaiah was written for the people of Israel who had been exiled, scattered across Mesopotamia after Judah's conquest by mighty Babylonia. These prophetic oracles were given to shape the worldview of the exiles, to provide a fresh founding narrative for the people of God. Thus, in this section of Isaiah one finds all the foundational stories of ancient Israel—creation, fall, election, slavery, exodus, covenant, land—all retold for the exiles of Israel, as if these captives were retracing the footsteps of their forefathers in their own experience of exile and return. Like their first forefather Adam, Israel has sinned against God (43:25–27), stripping God of the glory due him in their idolatry and injustice (e.g., 44:6–20). But the faithful God, the one and only Creator, is about to do something new, to re-create his people, the new children of Abraham, for his glory (e.g., 43:1–19). He has chosen a new servant, a new Moses, to lead them out of slavery in exile. This servant, paradoxically, is Israel itself and yet not-Israel—Israel embodied, perhaps—bringing about this new exodus to a new paradise through his self-giving suffering and death in anticipation of divine vindication (42:1–9; 44:1–5; 49:1–6; 50:4–10; especially 52:13—53:12). For this new people of God in this new creation there will be a new covenant, a fresh start in their relationship with God, enabled by the Spirit of God to do his will for his glory (e.g., 59:21).

In the midst of this epic drama of re-lived redemption, we find the language of "good news" in some prominent places. In the opening act God gives his messenger this charge:

> You who bring *good news* to Zion, go up on a high mountain. You who bring *good news* to Jerusalem, lift up your voice with a shout, lift it up, do not be afraid; say to the towns of Judah, "Here is your God!" See, the Sovereign Lord comes with power, and his arm rules for him. See, his reward is with him, and his recompense accompanies him. He tends his flock like a shepherd: He gathers the lambs in his arms and carries them close to his heart; he gently leads those that have young.
> (Isaiah 40:9–11, emphasis added)

This "good news," at its core, is a simple message: God is coming to his people. In spite of his apparent unfaithfulness, and in spite of their actual unfaithfulness, God has not abandoned them.

As this re-lived drama unfolds, the new Moses is introduced, God's servant, Israel embodied. This servant will accomplish God's purposes for his people and even for the nations, restoring Israel from captivity and exile and bringing the light of God's salvation to the ends of the earth. This motif is then expanded with the language of "good news":

> How beautiful on the mountains are the feet of those who bring *good news*, who proclaim peace, who bring *good news*, who proclaim salvation, who say to Zion, "Your God reigns!" Listen! Your watchmen lift up their voices; together they shout for joy. When the Lord returns to Zion, they will see it with their own eyes. Burst into songs of joy together, you ruins of Jerusalem, for the Lord has comforted his people, he has redeemed Jerusalem. The Lord will lay bare his holy arm in the sight of all the nations, and all the ends of the earth will see the salvation of our God.
> (Isaiah 52:7–10, emphasis added)

Here again, the "good news" is that God is coming to his people, but this is expanded in two crucial and integrally related ways: God comes to establish his supreme rule, and this means deliverance for the people of God. Thus, the light which the servant is to bring to Israel and the nations is that God's saving sovereignty has arrived. However, immediately following this declaration is an utterly astounding revelation: God will accomplish his saving sovereignty on earth, not through the power and might of the servant, but through the servant's obedient suffering and death. The servant, Israel embodied, will suffer and die for the sins of Israel, and through this act of the self-giving servant God will come to his people, revealing God's salvation and re-asserting God's sovereignty (Isaiah 52:13—53:12).

The goal of this re-lived drama of redemption is God's new work: the new people of God in a new creation living under a new covenant. In this Spirit-filled life, the accursed effects of sin and disobedience are reversed: the exiled captives are released, the oppressed poor are cared for, the long-suffering mourners are comforted. There are few passages in these latter oracles of Isaiah that state this as profoundly as this final "good news" passage:

> The Spirit of the Sovereign Lord is on me, because the Lord has anointed me to proclaim *good news* to the poor. He has sent me to bind up the brokenhearted, to proclaim freedom for the captives and release from darkness for the prisoners, to proclaim the year of the Lord's favor and the day of vengeance of our God, to comfort all who mourn, and provide for those who grieve in Zion—to bestow on them a crown of beauty instead of ashes, the oil of joy instead of mourning, and a garment of praise instead of a spirit of despair. They will be called mighty oaks, a planting of the Lord for the display of his splendor.
> (Isaiah 61:1–3, emphasis added)

Thus, these oracles of Isaiah draw on the foundational stories of the Jewish Scriptures to create an ornate tapestry of "good news": through the obedience and suffering of God's servant, Israel embodied, the faithful God will come to his unfaithful, exiled, and oppressed people, bringing new-covenant and new-creation deliverance to them and to the nations, and establishing his rightful sovereign rule over all his creation. This rich drama of re-lived redemption for God's exiled people resonated with many subsequent readers of Isaiah, but none as deeply as the first followers of Jesus, who saw this gospel story re-lived yet again in the life, death, and resurrection of Jesus of Nazareth.

CR

Another ancient "gospel" we need to explore is the "gospel" according to Rome. Around the time of the birth of Jesus, during the reign of the Emperor Augustus, the following message was inscribed in stone in prominent places throughout the Roman province of Asia Minor, giving reasons in support of an official change in the calendar system:

> Since the Providence that has divinely ordered our existence has applied her energy and zeal and has brought to life the most perfect good in Augustus, whom she filled with virtues for the benefit of humankind, bestowing him upon us and our descendants as a Savior, he who put an end to war and will order peace, Caesar, who by his appearance exceeded the hopes of those who prophesied *good news*, not only outdoing benefactors of the past, but also allowing no hope of greater benefactions in the future; and since the birthday of the god first brought to the world the *good news* residing in him . . . with good fortune and safety, the Greeks of Asia have decided that the New Year in all the cities should begin on 23rd September, the birthday of Augustus. (emphasis added)

This is only one prominent example of the sort of imperial propaganda one encountered in the first century AD. The Roman Emperors, particularly those judged after the fact to have been good for the Empire, could be described according to a stock narrative. Their birth was foretold by heavenly signs, their accession was marked by providential portents, their accomplishments were acts of the divine genius, their royal visits were as the arrival of the gods, and their death was their full entrance into deity. All of these were potential elements of "good news" insofar as they contributed to the greatest of Roman goals: peace and security for the many, bringing ease and comfort for the privileged few. Of course, this perpetual pursuit of peace and continual quest for comfort could only happen on the backs of the conquered, the enslaved, the oppressed, the over-taxed, the impoverished, the shamed, the crucified. This was the "gospel" of Rome's spin doctors: peace through conquest, security through oppression, salvation through crucifixion—for the glory of Rome and its Lord and Savior, Caesar.

The language of this Roman imperial propaganda was prominent enough to make early Christian ignorance of it quite unlikely. The first followers of Jesus knew very well what they were doing when they described Jesus as Messianic King, Lord, and Son of God; they were well aware of the implications of recounting his birth, life, and especially his Roman crucifixion and vindicating resurrection as "good news" of divine salvation and universal sovereignty. But what was the accession of another human Emperor, or the temporary peace of a troubled region, compared with the coming of the one true Lord and Savior to set the world right, bringing eternal peace and lasting deliverance from oppression, evil, and even death?

And so, the first followers of Jesus clashed with those who tolerated or embraced Rome's "gospel" vision. According to Acts, the Jerusalem apostles clashed with the Jewish religious elite who aligned themselves with Rome's power and believed that in doing so they could maintain the status quo and set the stage for the kingdom of God (e.g., Acts 4). Paul the apostle to the Gentiles clashed with imperialists in the non-Jewish world, those who professed absolute loyalty to Caesar as Lord and who could thus not tolerate any other royal claim (e.g., Acts 17:1–9). The gospel of Jesus thus undermined the myth of Rome, proclaiming the paradoxical foolishness that true divine sovereignty and salvation have been supremely manifested in the shameful crucifixion of an itinerant Galilean prophet at the hands of Rome and the ruling elite. The cross was thus an act of divine irony, in which Jesus submitted himself to the pre-eminent "gospel" of his age and so brought about the gospel of God; the resurrection was an act of divine reversal, in which Jesus enacted the gospel of God and so exposed the inadequacy of the "gospels" of the world.

❧

These three "gospels"—the primitive "gospel creed" focused on the resurrection of the crucified Jesus, the "gospel" of Isaiah, and the "gospel" of Rome—converged to shape the early Christians' understanding and expression of the gospel. But these did not all shape the Christian gospel in the same way, nor to the same degree. One could say that the Scriptures provided the content of the gospel, the expectation of what the "good news" should entail: the coming of God, the universal reign of God, the deliverance and restoration of the people of God and God's creation. The story of Jesus and his death and resurrection provided the agent and the means by which the gospel has been achieved in fulfillment of this Scriptural expectation: in Jesus—in his life and career, and supremely through his death "for our sins" and his resurrection "on the third day"—God has arrived on the scene, the sovereignty of God has been re-claimed, and the deliverance and restoration of creation and humanity has begun and will be fulfilled. And the Roman imperial propaganda provided a foil for the gospel, a significant part of the context in which the gospel was to be proclaimed and lived out: the gospel of God in Jesus confronts any counter-claims to universal salvation and sovereignty, subverting the values of this age with the values of the coming age that is already here, calling the evil powers of the world to account and its people to repent.

To be sure, the various New Testament authors provide different accounts of the gospel: the "gospel according to John" is not the same as that which Paul calls "my gospel," which in turn is different from the "gospel according to Matthew," and so on. The unifying, central gospel elements—Jesus, his death, and his resurrection, all understood in light of the Jewish Scriptures—were fleshed out in a variety of specific ways by the early Christians, an acceptable diversity that was generally a matter of emphasis in interpretation and expression. Mark's Gospel emphasizes Jesus as Messiah and thus describes the gospel more in terms of the "kingdom of God," God's saving sovereignty over humanity and creation brought about ultimately through Jesus' suffering and death. The writings of John especially highlight Jesus' unique Sonship and so in part describe the gospel in terms of people being re-born into God's new human family. Paul's teaching on "justification" focuses on Jesus' death as atoning and redeeming sacrifice for sin and his resurrection as a divine vindication in which believers participate. The book of Revelation strongly emphasizes Jesus' death as victory over the world's evil powers and as a pattern of righteous suffering for believers to follow, and Jesus' resurrection as the key which unlocks the final renewal of humanity and all creation. And this is only a sample of the gospel diversity reflected in the New Testament writings.

But the basic gospel portrait was remarkably uniform among the earliest Christians, and so should it also be for us today: God has decisively acted through Jesus of Nazareth, who is Messiah, Lord, and Son of God, particularly through Jesus' salvific death and resurrection, to make right everything that has gone wrong with the world because of sin. Thus the gospel is much bigger than many Christians think: individual sinners have their sins forgiven, experiencing deliverance from the corruption of sin, the pain and futility of human existence, the shame and hostility and oppression of broken relationships, the terror and exclusion of death; a new humanity is created, a diverse people united in Christ by God's Spirit in a new-covenant relationship with God; the evil powers of this age, whether unjust rulers or oppressive ideologies or the deep powers of sin and death, are nullified and in due course will be eradicated; all creation is liberated from the curse of sin to fulfill the purpose for which God created it. In short, God has entered his sin-scarred creation in Jesus, delivering humanity and all his creation from sin and all its consequences, and re-establishing his faithful and loving sovereignty among humanity and all creation. All this has already begun through

Jesus, through his life, death, and resurrection, and all this will one day be completed at his return.

∞

Belief in this good news of salvation through the crucified and resurrected Jesus, trust in God the Father acting through his Son Jesus to bring about his good purposes for creation, loyal dependence upon the loving and faithful God patterned after Jesus' own relationship to the Father—all this is encapsulated in one significant word: *faith*.

For the early Christians it was this faith in the faithful God through the faithful Jesus, this basic gospel narrative of Jesus crucified and resurrected, that lay behind two distinctive rituals: baptism and the Eucharist. By being baptized, normally in earliest Christianity through full immersion in water, the believer signified his or her individual participation in the gospel story of Jesus' death, burial, and resurrection, being "buried with Jesus through baptism" and raised to "new life" (Romans 6:4)—a baptismal tradition held not just by Paul but also by other early Christians (Romans 6:17). By celebrating the Eucharist (the Lord's Supper or Communion), the local community of believers signified their collective participation in this gospel story, eating and drinking "in remembrance" of Jesus and "proclaiming his death" (1 Corinthians 11:24–26)— a Eucharistic tradition held not just by Paul but also by other early Christians (1 Corinthians 11:23). And so, every time these two most significant, historic rituals of Christianity are performed, Christians faithfully re-enact the foundational gospel story centered on the crucified and resurrected Jesus, they re-trace that first journey of the first followers of Jesus in reflecting on the significance of Jesus, his death, and his resurrection.

After reading . . .

- What is the gospel? In view of the biblical texts listed below, do you think the summary provided in this chapter is an accurate or complete description of the gospel?

- How is the death and resurrection of Jesus "good news"?

- How does the broader biblical context help define the gospel?

- How did the contemporary context of the early Christians shape their understanding and expression of the gospel? How should our context today contribute to the way we understand and express the gospel?

- What is "faith"? How might this faith be practiced in your own life?

- What does it mean to say that baptism and the Eucharist are "re-enactments of the foundational gospel story"?

For further reading . . .

BIBLICAL TEXTS:

Isaiah 40, 42, 49, 52–53, 61; Mark 1, 8, 14–16; John 3; Acts 2, 10, 13; Romans 3–8, 10; 1 Corinthians 1–2, 15; 1 Peter 1–2; 1 John 3–4.

Hengel, Martin. *The Four Gospels and the One Gospel of Jesus Christ: An Investigation of the Collection and Origin of the Canonical Gospels.* London: SCM Press, 2000.

Includes a thorough discussion of the concept of "gospel" in earliest Christianity and its focus on Jesus, his death, and his resurrection.

Stanton, Graham. *Jesus and Gospel*. Cambridge: Cambridge University Press, 2004.

Includes a thorough discussion of the concept of "gospel" in earliest Christianity within its Jewish and Greco-Roman contexts, including its focus on Jesus, his death, and his resurrection.

Wright, N. T. *The New Testament and the People of God*. Minneapolis: Fortress, 1992.

A scholarly discussion which includes a thoughtful exploration of the significance of the story of Jesus for early Christian thought and practice.

5

Father

Before you read . . .

- Why do you believe in God?

- How would you describe God?

- What qualities come to mind when you think of the word "father"?

AT THIS POINT our journey takes a turn. We move from the central beliefs of Christianity summarized in the gospel, to the most significant beliefs which flow directly out of those core gospel convictions. After all, the early Christian belief in Jesus' resurrection not only impacted Christian perspectives on Jesus' death, the identity of Jesus, and the nature of salvation. The resurrection of the crucified Jesus also changed the way the earliest Christians thought and talked about God, humanity, and all creation.

In Jesus, a new story of God was told, causing all who heard it to re-think the earlier stories that had been told about God. These earlier stories, found in the narratives and poetry and prophecies of ancient Israel, are familiar from our journey so far. Three foundational descriptions of God emerge from these stories, forming a crucial framework for all subsequent Jewish conceptions of God.

The first of these foundational descriptions is *God as Creator*. God is the one who made time and space and filled it with his creatures, calling his creation "very good" (Genesis 1:31). God sustains the creation through constant, providential care, and moves creation toward God's good purposes for it. This foundational description of God speaks of God's transcendence, the "utter beyondness" of God, and God's holiness, or "complete otherness"—the Creator alone is God, and all else is not-God. As the transcendent Creator, God is omnipotent or all-powerful; God alone "calls into being things that were not" (Romans 4:17). This foundational description of God also speaks of God's immanence, the "intimate nearness" of God. As the immanent Creator, God is omniscient and omnipresent, knowing everything and being everywhere. Because God is utterly beyond created time and space, completely other in relation to the creation, God can also wholly permeate the created order. And it is in this immanence that God shows his faithfulness and his love to his creation, devotedly caring for it as a mother cares for her newborn baby, maintaining that devotion even when that infant grows into a wayward child.

A second foundational description of God in the Jewish Scriptures is *God as Ruler*. This is especially expressed in terms of God as "King" and as "Lord," themes we have already explored. It is even implicit in the simple description of God as "God," the powerful deity to whom God's people owe allegiance. God the Creator is of necessity God the Ruler, the rightful owner over creation and therefore sovereign over the earth and its people. All creation, all people, and in particular those people who call him their God—all owe their existence to God and so also their loyalty, submitting to the divine purposes for their existence. This foundational description of God re-emphasizes God's transcendence and holiness. God the Ruler is the "utterly beyond" God, the "completely other" God, who governs creation through the sovereign execution of his will, and judges the creation as he sees fit.

A third foundational description of God in the Scriptures of ancient Israel is *God as Covenant-Keeper*. The narratives of the Jewish Scriptures tell of several covenants God makes with various people. Some are no more than promises on God's part to act in certain ways on behalf of the other party, but some are more formal agreements outlining the responsibilities and privileges inherent in the relationship.

One important covenant example is from the Abraham stories of Genesis. God promises to Abraham that he will make a great nation from him and his descendants, blessing him in order that all peoples of the earth will be blessed (Genesis 12:1–3). This promise is formalized as a covenant in a later narrative, as God again promises to do all this for Abraham, with Abraham and his descendants marking themselves as participants in this special relationship by the outward sign of male circumcision (Genesis 15, 17). Another prominent covenant is found further on in the books of Moses, especially Exodus and Deuteronomy. According to these accounts, God redeems these descendants of Abraham from slavery in Egypt, leading them in their exodus from the land of their enemies, and through mighty acts of deliverance brings them to Mount Sinai. There God establishes a formal covenant with the people of Israel through Moses, outlining the history of his care for them, listing their covenant responsibilities in the Ten Commandments and other related laws, and describing his covenant responsibilities in terms of blessings for the people of Israel if they remain faithful to the covenant (Exodus 19–24; Deuteronomy).

These two covenants were the ones most on the minds of the Jewish people in the time of Jesus. They were the children of Abraham, to be blessed by God in the promised land, marked off from all other peoples by the sign of male circumcision. They were the keepers of Torah, the people of God redeemed and established by God through Moses, marked off from all other peoples by their adherence to the Mosaic covenant and its laws. So it was natural for these two covenants to be the lens through which the people understood the promise of the biblical prophets that God would establish a new covenant with his people, fulfilling the promises to Abraham and Moses of a people blessed by God, fulfilling the will of God.

This foundational description of God as Covenant-Keeper re-emphasizes God's immanence, God's intimate "nearness." God may be the transcendent God, but he desires to draw near to his human creation in relationship; God may be the all-sovereign, all-powerful Ruler, but God does not force the divine will on humanity, instead choosing to draw humanity to himself in loving, caring relationship—even to the extent of wrapping up his very identity with the identity of his people, as "the God of Abraham, Isaac, and Jacob" (e.g. Exodus 3:6).

∞

For the early Christians, all three of these foundational descriptions of God from the Jewish Scriptures were encapsulated in one term: *Father*. The ancient Mediterranean world was a patriarchal society, meaning among other things that the father of a family was viewed as having an established, foundational role in the family and in broader society. In both Jewish and broader Greco-Roman society of Jesus' day, the ideals of fatherhood included a few key concepts: *origin*, the father as the source of his family; *authority*, the father as the head over his family; and *care*, the father as the provider and protector of his family. These are, in essence, the key concepts underlying God as Creator, God as Ruler, and God as Covenant-Keeper—God as Father fills them all.

While the idea of God as Father is found in the Jewish Scriptures, it gained new momentum, even added meaning, in light of the life, death, and resurrection of Jesus. As we have already explored, there was a strong early Christian memory of Jesus calling God *Abba*, emphasizing the ideals of fatherhood in an especially personal and intimate way. This is further underscored in one early Christian story found in the Gospel of Luke, one of Jesus' best-known parables: the story of the Prodigal Son (Luke 15:11–32). This story is as much or more about the father as it is about the two sons, highlighting the father's willingness to let his sons choose their own path, his generosity to his sons even if he suspects one will go astray, his longing for his wayward son's return, his compassion and forgiveness and celebration for this son at his homecoming, his understanding yet firm resolve in the face of his older son's objections. God the Father—the origin of, authority over, and caregiver for all his creation—longs for the return of his human creatures to their intended purpose in intimate relationship with him.

As we have already noted, at least some early Christians such as Paul viewed Jesus' resurrection as the moment at which God appointed Jesus as his unique Son—and therefore God was uniquely his Father. This idea lies behind the common Pauline description of God as "the God and Father of our Lord Jesus Christ." The unique relationship of God the Father and the Son of God is what enables the renewed relationship of Christians as children of God the Father. As Paul declares in both Romans and Galatians, those who are "in Christ" are adopted as God's children and cry out to God as *Abba*—the very cry of Jesus to his Father echoing in the hearts of believers by his Spirit within them (Romans 8:15; Galatians 4:6). The writings of John also describe this reality: Jesus the Messiah is the "one and only" Son of God the Father, and it is through belief in him that people can become "children of God" (John 1:11–14).

All this should recall the creation story and the *imago Dei*—indeed, the beginning of John's Gospel explicitly points its readers back to creation "in the beginning" even as it describes the Sonship of Jesus and the derivative "sonship" of believers. God created humanity "in his image," to be his unique royal representatives in a unique filial relationship with him, uniquely reflecting his character as a child does his parents. Jesus, the unique Son of God, is the perfect "image of God," the exact representation of God in his kingship and character. And it is through Jesus that humanity can reclaim the promise of *imago Dei*, achieving these original creative purposes of God, "the Father of our Lord Jesus Christ." Paul summarizes this nicely in his letter to the Romans, affirming that "those who love [God], who have been called according to his purpose . . . [will] be conformed to the image of his Son, that he might be the firstborn among many brothers and sisters" (Romans 8:28–29)—a whole family crying out "*Abba*, Father."

Transcendence. Immanence. Holiness. Sovereignty. Love. Faithfulness. *Father*. All these ideas are brought together in the Lord's Prayer, the prayer remembered by Jesus' disciples as the pattern Jesus taught them for their own prayers to God, their *Abba*:

> Our Father in heaven, your name is holy.
> May your kingdom come, your will be done, on
>   earth as it is in heaven.
> Give us this day our daily bread.
> Forgive us our sins as we forgive those who sin
>   against us.
> Do not bring us to the time of testing, but deliver
>   us from evil.
> For the kingdom and the power and the glory are
>   yours forever. Amen.

❧

If you were to ask an ancient Israelite to explain God's power and his love, he or she would very likely tell you one of two stories: creation or the exodus. At least, this is the way the Jewish Scriptures describe these two dynamic attributes of God. The story of God creating what is out of what was not, and then caring for creation by providing everything needed for a blessed existence, emphasizes both God's mighty power and faithful love. The story of God redeeming the people of Israel from slavery in Egypt and delivering them from the

Egyptian army through a miraculous event, again highlights both God's faithful love and mighty power. These stories are repeatedly recalled in the Jewish Scriptures to underscore for Israel that their God is both powerful enough to sustain and assist them and caring enough to do so.

But for the earliest followers of Jesus—most of them Jews in the heritage of ancient Israel—these stories virtually disappeared as the first point of reference in describing God's power and love. A new story shaped the early Christian understanding of God's love and power: the crucifixion and resurrection of Jesus.

When the New Testament authors wanted to describe the power of God, they turned to Jesus' resurrection. So God's "incomparably great power for us who believe" is expanded in Ephesians as "the mighty strength he exerted when he raised Christ from the dead" (Ephesians 1:19–20). It is this resurrection power which effects salvation from sin, giving us "new birth into a living hope through the resurrection of Jesus Christ from the dead" (1 Peter 1:3), enabling believers to live a life of righteousness because we have been "raised with [Christ] through your faith in the working of God, who raised him from the dead" (Colossians 2:12). The stories of creation and exodus reverberate in the New Testament descriptions of Jesus' resurrection, pointing back to the motifs of transcendence in the foundational Jewish descriptions of God: God's power, holiness, and sovereignty over all creation.

And when the New Testament authors wanted to describe the love of God, they turned to Jesus' death. "God demonstrates his own love for us in this," Paul says, "While we were still sinners, Christ died for us" (Romans 5:8). Or, as 1 John echoes, "This is how we know what love is: Jesus Christ laid down his life for us" (1 John 3:16); and again, "This is how God showed his love among us: He sent his one and only Son into the world that we might live through him. This is love: not that we loved God, but that he loved us and sent his Son as an atoning sacrifice for our sins" (1 John 4:9–10). The stories of exodus and covenant reverberate in the New Testament descriptions of Jesus' crucifixion, pointing back to the motifs of immanence in the foundational Jewish descriptions of God: God's love, faithfulness, and intimate relationship with his people.

God, "the Father of our Lord Jesus Christ," is thus both the transcendent God who has displayed his powerful sovereignty through the resurrection of his Son Jesus, and the immanent God who has displayed his faithful love through the salvific death of his Son Jesus.

ॐ

Always nagging at the conscience of our conversations about God are some hard, deep questions about knowledge and reality: How do we even know God exists? And if God does exist, how can we know God? That is, how might we discern God's activity in the world in order to understand who God is? The early Christian answer to these sorts of questions was simple, yet profound: look to the crucified and resurrected Jesus.

While the New Testament authors affirm the common Jewish perspective that the created order, human history, and the Scriptures all function in different ways as disclosures of who God is or what God does, none of these is described as the ultimate revelation of God. Rather, in the New Testament this status is consistently ascribed only to Jesus. Jesus, through his life, death, and resurrection, is the definitive disclosure of God's nature, identity, and purposes.

This idea can be seen overtly in several New Testament passages. The author of Hebrews boldly asserts: "In the past God spoke to our ancestors through the prophets at many times and in various ways, but in these last days he has spoken to us by his Son, . . . the radiance of God's glory and the exact representation of his being" (Hebrews 1:1–3). In a similar way the opening of John's Gospel declares: "No one has ever seen God, but the one and only, who is himself God and is in closest relationship with the Father, has made him known" (John 1:18). But this idea that Jesus is God's ultimate self-revelation can also be seen more subtly in the New Testament writings. For example, Paul affirms in Romans not only that God is the God who "calls into being things that were not"—that is, the Creator—but that in light of Jesus' resurrection he has also shown himself to be "the God who gives life to the dead"—the Re-Creator, if you will (Romans 4:17). Or, in 1 Corinthians, Paul takes the foundational Jewish creed, the opening section of the *Shema* from Deuteronomy 6 which declares that "the Lord our God is one," and in light of the crucified and resurrected Jesus re-shapes this into a distinctively Christian creed: "There is but one God, the Father, from whom all things came and for whom we live; and there is but one Lord, Jesus Christ, through whom all things came and through whom we live" (1 Corinthians 8:6).

This concept of the crucified and resurrected Jesus as the ultimate revelation of God has several profound implications for the nagging questions of knowledge and reality. In response to the question, "How do we know that God exists?" the most basic Christian answer could well be, "Because God raised Jesus from the dead—and God's resurrection power continues to change lives, bringing life out of death." Of course, this answer is already a response of faith; that is, it will not convince someone of the existence of God who is not already predisposed to that belief, particularly in view of the reality discussed earlier that one cannot prove the resurrection of Jesus either by critical history or by analytical logic. Nevertheless, this is exactly what is called for in the Christian proclamation of the crucified and resurrected Jesus: a genuine response of faith and trust, not the false security of a claim to irrefutable knowledge.

So, "How might we discern God's activity in the world in order to understand who God is?" Again, the most basic Christian answer is bound up with the crucified and resurrected Jesus. As we have seen, the resurrection of the crucified Jesus points to Jesus as the embodiment of God, perfectly reflecting God's identity, purpose, actions, and character. Or, in the language of John's Gospel, Jesus the "one and only Son," the eternal "Word" who is fully God, became "enfleshed" or "incarnate" as a fully human being (John 1:14). Jesus, the ultimate revelation of God, is fully God and fully human—not half and half, not sometimes one and sometimes the other, but always and completely God and always and completely human. That this inexplicable, paradoxical, divine-human concurrence is at the heart of God's definitive self-disclosure in Jesus suggests that it is God's ideal mode of revelation. God's transcendence or "utter beyondness" and God's immanence or "intimate nearness" are perfectly united in Jesus, especially in his death and resurrection—and this paradoxical mix of transcendence and immanence reflects God's preferred way of acting in the natural world and through human history.

So we should not expect to find God only "in the gaps" of our knowledge of the natural world or human history. God is as much present in the scientifically and historically explainable as he is in that which has not yet been explained. Nor should we expect to see God only in the "miraculous," or in the triumphs of life. God is as much present in the mundane and in life's tragedies as he is in those experiences which are typically seen as the more likely demonstrations of divine activity.

God is, after all, the one who impossibly resurrected Jesus from the dead, just as he is the fully human, crucified God.

After reading . . .

- What are the three foundational descriptions of God in the Jewish Scriptures? How do these reflect God's transcendence and immanence? God's holiness, power, and love? How are these encapsulated in the designation of God as "Father"? In view of the biblical texts listed below, do you think these together provide an accurate or complete description of who God is?

- How does the Lord's Prayer reflect these ideas of who God is? How might these ideas affect the way you pray?

- What is the ultimate demonstration of God's love? of God's power? How does this affect the way you understand God's love and power in your life?

- What is "the most basic Christian answer" to the question of God's existence? What are some possible difficulties with this answer? What are some advantages of this answer? Do you think we can ever satisfactorily "solve" the "problem" of God's existence?

For further reading . . .

BIBLICAL TEXTS:

Genesis 1, 12, 15; Exodus 19–24; Deuteronomy; Luke 15; John 1; Romans 5, 8; Ephesians 1–3; Colossians 1; Hebrews 1; 1 John 4.

Bauckham, Richard. *Jesus and the God of Israel: God Crucified and Other Studies on the New Testament's Christology of Divine Identity.* Grand Rapids: Eerdmans, 2008.

A thorough exploration of the significance of Jesus' life, death, and resurrection for understanding the nature of God.

Moltmann, Jürgen. *The Crucified God: The Cross of Christ as the Foundation and Criticism of Christian Theology.* London: SCM Press, 1974.

A scholarly exploration of the significance of Jesus' crucifixion for understanding the nature of God and broader Christian theology.

Wright, N. T. *Jesus and the Victory of God.* Minneapolis: Fortress, 1996.

A scholarly exploration of Jesus' life which includes discussion of the way in which Jesus "embodied" and revealed God through his life and death.

————. *The New Testament and the People of God.* Minneapolis: Fortress, 1992.

A scholarly presentation which includes discussion of early Christian understandings of the identity of God in the context of early Jewish perspectives.

6

Spirit

Before you read . . .

- What comes to mind when you think of the word "spirit"?
- Why do you think the Holy Spirit is necessary for Christian theology and living the Christian life? What does the Holy Spirit do?

BOTH THE HEBREW (*ruach*) and the Greek (*pneuma*) words for "spirit" also mean "wind" or "breath." While one should be careful about making too much of this correlation, it is not without significance. After all, there are several places in the biblical writings where the analogy between "spirit" and "wind" is directly drawn, even in a play on words. Perhaps the best known of these is in John's Gospel, where Jesus is described as saying to Nicodemus, "The wind (*pneuma*) blows wherever it pleases. You hear its sound, but you cannot tell where it comes from or where it is going. So it is with everyone born of the Spirit (*pneuma*)" (John 3:8). The wind is an often unpredictable force that itself cannot be seen, but is only discernible by its effects on other things: the rustling of leaves, the swaying of branches. So it is with the Spirit of God: invisible, powerful, effective—and often unpredictable. Yet, like an unexpected breeze in the scorching heat of a desert, or like a surprising wind that brings much-needed rains to a thirsty land, so God's Spirit can bring refreshment, even life.

These sorts of motifs are reiterated throughout the Jewish Scriptures related to God's Spirit. Yet just as the resurrection of the crucified Jesus changed the way his first followers thought about God, so this event transformed the way the earliest Christians conceived of God's Spirit.

CR

As we have seen, the resurrection of Jesus was an eschatological event, a "renewal." Jesus' resurrection marked the time of the eschaton, announcing that the era of the fulfillment of God's promises had arrived. And one of these crucial promises to be fulfilled was the promise of the outpouring of God's Spirit on the people of God at the time of the end, a mark of the new covenant God was to make with them.

The story of Pentecost in Acts highlights this, as Peter's sermon opens with this quotation from the oracles of the biblical prophet Joel:

> In the last days, God says, I will pour out my Spirit on all people. Your sons and daughters will prophesy, your young men will see visions, your old men will dream dreams. Even on my servants, both men and women, I will pour out my Spirit in those days, and they will prophesy.
> (Acts 2:17–18; see Joel 2:28–29)

The original passage in Joel was part of a promise of what God would do when he restored the people from their exile, gathering them from among the nations. While God's Spirit had been active in the world since creation, the Spirit of God would do something new at this time of eschatological fulfillment.

Similar promises in other Old Testament prophetic writings make explicit the idea that this restoration by God's Spirit would include a new covenant, a new relationship between God and God's people. Jeremiah spoke of a "new covenant" between God and the people, with God's Law "in their minds" and "on their hearts," with all God's people knowing God in fully forgiven intimacy (Jeremiah 31:31–34). Ezekiel also prophesied about this future restoration, describing a "new heart" and a "new spirit," God's Spirit, placed within God's people to enable them to keep God's laws (Ezekiel 36:24–28). And Isaiah predicted a similar reality at this eschatological time of renewal, declaring that this future covenant would mean that God's Spirit would never depart from among God's people (Isaiah 59:21).

Three features of the eschatological, new-covenant Spirit of God are especially prominent in these sorts of biblical prophecies and particularly highlighted in the New Testament descriptions of God's Spirit. First, *the new-covenant Spirit of God enables God's people to know God in intimate relationship.* As the passage from Jeremiah indicates, this personal knowledge of God would not merely be reserved for priests and prophets, but all of God's people, "from the least to the greatest," would know God personally and intimately. This idea is behind the descriptions of "re-birth" or "regeneration" in the New Testament writings. For example, Jesus' call to

Nicodemus to be "born again" or "born of the Spirit" is a call to enter into this promised new relationship with God, to be made new by the refreshing winds of God's Spirit (John 3:3, 5, 8). In several places Paul describes Gentile Christians as those who once did not know God but now do know God as part of this new covenant with him, and it is Paul's fervent prayer that they would "grow in the knowledge of God." Thus, Jews and Gentiles together are heirs of this new-covenant promise, together entering this new relationship with God; as Paul asserts, "we were all baptized by one Spirit so as to form one body—whether Jews or Gentiles, slave or free—and we were all given the one Spirit to drink" (1 Corinthians 12:13).

Second, *the new-covenant Spirit of God enables God's people to fulfill God's will in acts of love.* This appears in several of the Old Testament prophecies quoted above, particularly in the idea of God's Law being "written on the hearts" of God's people with God's Spirit prompting his people to follow the divine decrees. The broader contexts of these prophetic passages tend to focus on two areas in which God's will needs to be fulfilled: bringing justice for the oppressed and marginalized, and showing mercy to the needy and the lowly. As we have seen, this sort of justice and mercy was exemplified by Jesus in his life and death, a complete self-giving for the benefit of others, even for those viewed by the world as the last, the least, and the lost—a self-giving summed up in the word "love." This is also the way the Spirit-filled believers are described in the early chapters of the book of Acts: bringing in to the community of God's people those who were on the margins, sharing with all those who had need. As Paul highlights in both Romans and Galatians, it is by the Spirit that Christians truly love others, and so fulfill "the righteous requirement of the Law" (Romans 8:3–4; 13:9–10; Galatians 5:13–26).

Third, *the new-covenant Spirit of God enables God's people to perform God's mighty acts of deliverance in the world.* Luke's Gospel especially portrays Jesus' public career in this way. He proclaims God's message and heals people "by the Spirit of God," and so demonstrates that the time of eschatological fulfillment has arrived. Luke's second volume, Acts, continues this idea but applies it to God's Spirit-filled people. The apostles in particular proclaim God's message of salvation through the resurrected Jesus and perform extraordinary acts of healing by the Spirit. Paul even goes so far as to say that such "signs, wonders, and miracles" are the "marks of a true apostle," one truly sent by Jesus to be his representative (2 Corinthians 12:12). Because the time of fulfillment has arrived in Jesus the people of God empowered by the Spirit of God can do the mighty salvific works of God: proclaiming the message of God's salvation, living out this salvation, and providing a foretaste of its ultimate fulfillment.

☙

For the earliest Christians, the resurrection of the crucified Jesus not only marked the beginning of the eschaton and thus the fulfillment of the new-covenant promise of God's Spirit for God's people. The resurrection of the crucified Jesus also shaped the early Christian understanding of precisely who the Spirit is: the new-covenant Spirit of God is in fact the Spirit of Christ. So in Romans 8:9–10 Paul can move without apology or explanation between "Spirit of God," "Spirit of Christ," and even "Christ" as the one who dwells within and among believers, marking them off as God's people and enabling them to fulfill God's will. Similar identification of the Spirit as the Spirit of Jesus can be seen elsewhere in the New Testament (e.g., Acts 16:7; 1 Peter 1:11). The crucified and resurrected Jesus has ascended to the very presence of the Father; yet, as the earliest Christians personally experienced in their worship and their daily life, Jesus continues to be present among his people by his Spirit.

There are at least two significant ideas that flow out of this early Christian identification of the Spirit of God as the Spirit of Christ. First, *as the Spirit of Christ, the Holy Spirit shapes God's people individually and collectively into the image of the crucified and resurrected Jesus.* As we have seen at several points in our journey thus far, Jesus as the Messiah and Son of God fulfills the promise inherent in the *imago Dei*, as the royal Messiah bringing in God's kingdom on earth, and as the Son in unique relationship with God the Father, embodying God's identity and character to the world. Jesus is not merely created "in the image of God"; he *is* the "image of God" (Colossians 1:15; see Hebrews 1:3). And so the Spirit of Christ within and among believers shapes them into the image of Christ, prompting Christ-like faith, hope, and love, and so fulfilling the promise of *imago Dei* for all humanity. This, in Paul's words, is the very "purpose" of God for humanity: to be "conformed to the image of his Son" (Romans 8:28–30).

There were several metaphors used by the earliest Christians to describe how the Spirit shapes believers into the image of Christ. One of Paul's favorite images was the idea of "walking" in the Spirit (Galatians 5:16–26). This metaphor comes out of his Jewish training and worldview, reflecting the language of *halakah* or instructions about how to "walk" in the Law of Moses and so fulfill God's will. For Paul, how-ever, one "walks" in the Spirit to be shaped into God's will of Christ-likeness. Christ-likeness is not achieved overnight, but by a lifetime of small steps toward the goal. Another metaphor for this work of the Spirit used especially by Paul and Luke is the image of the Spirit's "filling" (Acts 2:4; 4:31; Ephesians 5:18). Being "filled with the Spirit" brings to mind similar phrases such as being "filled with fear" or "filled with joy," the idea that one is so consumed by fear or joy that for a time this emotion compels one to think and act in a certain way. Like the wind that "fills" the sails of a ship, so the Spirit of Christ "fills" the follower of Christ, compelling him or her to think and act like the crucified and resurrected Jesus. Christ-likeness is not achieved by a set of rules, but by carefully con-sidering the image of Christ and being compelled by his Spirit to reflect that image. As Paul says, "we all, who with unveiled faces contemplate the Lord's glory, are being transformed into his image with ever-increasing glory, which comes from the Lord, who is the Spirit" (2 Corinthians 3:18).

A second idea flows from the notion that the Spirit of God is the Spirit of Christ: *as the Spirit of Christ, the Holy Spirit witnesses to Christ, directing people to the crucified and resurrected Jesus.* As Jesus in John's Gospel declares to his disciples, "When the Advocate comes, whom I will send to you from the Father—the Spirit of truth who goes out from the Father—he will testify about me" (John 15:26). The New Testament writings describe two main ways the Spirit wit-nesses to the crucified and risen Christ: through written Scripture, and through God's people.

For the New Testament authors, "Scripture" or "the Scriptures" referred to the Jewish Scriptures, the collection of sacred writings roughly equivalent to the Christian Old Testament and, for most first-century Jews, thought of as divided into three groupings: the Law of Moses, the Prophets, and the Writings. According to the earliest Christians, it is these Scriptures which witness to the gospel of the crucified and resurrected Jesus; or, in the words of the primitive gospel tradition cited by Paul and shared by the other apostles and witnesses, Jesus' death "for our sins" and his resurrection "on the third day" are both "according to the Scriptures" (1 Corinthians 15:3–4). Other early Christians also indicate this gospel witness by Scripture: the Scriptures themselves do not give eternal life, but they witness to Jesus who alone brings life (John 5:39–40); Moses and the Prophets and all the Scriptures testify to Christ's suffering and glory (Luke 24:26–27); the Law and the Prophets bear witness to God's saving action in Christ (Romans 3:21–26); the Spirit of Christ within the Prophets predicted the sufferings of Christ and the glories to follow (1 Peter 1:10–11); indeed, the very purpose of these sacred writings is to make one wise for salvation through Christ Jesus (2 Timothy 3:15).

This last passage goes on to affirm that "All Scripture is God-breathed (or inspired by God, *theopneustos*) and is useful for teaching, rebuking, correcting and training in righteousness" (2 Timothy 3:16–17). As this statement has played a crucial role in developing Christian perspectives on the nature and purpose of Scripture, it is worth pausing to look more closely at it in light of our journey so far. The key term *theopneustos* is not found anywhere else in the biblical writings; indeed, it appears to have been coined for just this occasion. While there is much debate over the precise meaning of the word, I would suggest that the idea of "God-breathed" or "inspired" is intended to recall an ancient biblical story, the account of God's creation of Adam: "Then the Lord God formed a man from the dust of the ground and breathed into his nostrils the breath of life, and the man became a living being" (Genesis 2:7). In this narrative, God creates Adam by shaping earthly matter and breathing into it to make someone living and active; in a similar way, God worked through human authors, "breathing into" their writings to make an "alive and active" Scripture (see Hebrews 4:12). This echoes our discussion in the previous chapter that, in light of God's ultimate self-revelation in Christ, God's preferred mode of revelation is a paradoxical, divine-human concurrence. As we saw in the first stages of our journey, the written Scriptures—human writings somehow "breathed into" by God's Spirit—provide a divinely originating and authoritative witness to the crucified and resurrected Jesus. These Old Testament Scriptures are like the early chapters of a well-written story which introduce setting, characters, and motifs that find their satisfactory conclusion in the book's final chapters.

There is another way in which the Holy Spirit witnesses to Christ: through God's people. United to Christ by his Spirit, then empowered by the Spirit of Christ, God's people proclaim the gospel of the crucified and resurrected Jesus, and live out the pattern of the crucified and risen Jesus. These sorts of ideas are found throughout the New Testament writings in various ways. The Acts narrative repeatedly describes the bold witness of the earliest Christians as they were "filled with the Spirit." So, for example, they prayed to God, "enable your servants to speak your word with great boldness," and as a result they were "filled with the Holy Spirit and spoke the word of God boldly" (Acts 4:29–31). Paul also made a strong connection between his preaching of the gospel and the power of the Spirit. He proclaimed the gospel "not simply with words but also with power, with the Holy Spirit and with deep conviction" (1 Thessalonians 1:5). Similarly, John's Gospel makes the connection between the witness of the Spirit to Jesus and the witness of his followers. The "Spirit of truth," sent by the Father and by Jesus in his name, is to teach Jesus' followers by reminding them of what he taught them, and through this to "testify" to Jesus alongside those followers who have "been with [him] from the beginning" (John 14:26; 15:26–27). Finally, Paul especially describes the role of the Spirit within believers living out the pattern of Jesus' death and resurrection as a witness to the world. For example, it is by the Spirit of Christ that one can "put to death the misdeeds of the body" and by which "life" is given to "mortal bodies" (Romans 8:9–14), and it is by the new-covenant Spirit that even one's faithfulness in hardship and suffering can be a testimony to the death and resurrection of Jesus (2 Corinthians 3–4).

While all Christians testify to Christ by his Spirit in these ways, there was one group of people who were especially noted in the earliest Christian writings as witnesses to Jesus through their gospel preaching and living: the "apostles." These were people generally considered by the first Christians to be special envoys of Jesus, personally commissioned by him to be his authoritative representatives in speech and action. The core of this group was twelve men who had been with Jesus throughout his public ministry, each of which was in particular "a witness . . . of his resurrection" (Acts 1:21–26). Paul considered himself among these "apostles" by virtue of his personal encounter with and commission by the resurrected Jesus, a consideration confirmed by other apostles (Galatians 1–2). The New Testament writings by and large are the writings of these apostles and their close associates, and thus they reflect this unique apostolic witness to Christ enabled by his Spirit: authoritatively telling Jesus' story, relating Jesus' teachings, interpreting Jesus' death and resurrection, testifying to Jesus' identity and mission. And it is for this reason that the New Testament writings have been rightly considered Scripture by Christians, just as much the divinely authoritative, Spirit-inspired witness to Christ as the Old Testament writings are.

CR

There is much that remains a mystery about the Spirit. How can we discern the genuine activity of the Spirit in the midst of a myriad of different claims of the Spirit's activity? Exactly how does the Spirit work to shape the people of God into the image of Christ? How similar and how different can this process be for individual believers, or for particular communities? How should we describe the work of the Spirit in the production of Scripture? These kinds of questions have produced a variety of answers throughout Christian history. But this sort of mystery surrounding the Spirit should come as no surprise. After all, trying to discern the Spirit is like grasping at the wind, something invisible, powerful, effective, and often unpredictable; yet God's people must yield to this mysterious Spirit, the breath of God, in order to find life in the crucified and risen Jesus.

After reading . . .

- What does it mean to say that the Holy Spirit is the "new-covenant Spirit"? What does it mean to say that the Holy Spirit is the "Spirit of Christ"? In view of the biblical texts listed below, do you think these provide an accurate or complete description of who the Holy Spirit is and what the Spirit does?

- How does the Holy Spirit "witness to Christ" through Scripture? How should an understanding of Scripture as "God-breathed" or "inspired" affect the way we read Scripture and respond to it?

- How does the Holy Spirit "witness to Christ" through God's people? What might this look like in your world?

For further reading . . .

Biblical texts: Jeremiah 31; Ezekiel 36–37; John 3, 5, 15; Acts 1–2; Romans 8; 1 Corinthians 12; Galatians 5; 2 Timothy 3; 1 Peter 1.

Dunn, James D. G. *Jesus and the Spirit: A Study of the Religious and Charismatic Experience of Jesus and the First Christians as Reflected in the New Testament.* Philadelphia: Westminster, 1975.

A scholarly study of Jesus' and his first followers' experience and understanding of God's Spirit.

Fee, Gordon D. *God's Empowering Presence: The Holy Spirit in the Letters of Paul.* Peabody, MA: Hendrickson, 1994.

A detailed study of the passages in Paul's letters that speak of the identity and significance of the Holy Spirit.

———. *Paul, the Spirit, and the People of God.* Peabody, MA: Hendrickson, 1996.

A shorter, accessible treatment of Paul's teaching on the identity and significance of the Holy Spirit.

Turner, Max. *The Holy Spirit and Spiritual Gifts: Then and Now.* Carlisle, Cumbria: Paternoster, 1996.

An exploration of the Christian doctrine of pneumatology, including the Holy Spirit's nature and activity among God's people.

7

Creation

Before you read . . .

- What comes to mind when you hear the word "creation"?

- What do you think distinguishes humankind from the rest of creation? What do humans hold in common with all creation?

- What comes to mind when you hear the word "church"? How might it relate to the word "creation"?

MANY CHRISTIANS TODAY focus on the "when" and the "how" of creation, how old the earth is and the way in which it was created. But the Christian Scriptures instead focus on the "who" and the "why" of creation, questions which find their answers in terrain we have already explored—God the Father and Creator, the *imago Dei*, the gospel—answers which are all affirmed in the resurrection of the crucified Jesus.

As we have seen, God the Creator made all that is not-God, showing God's transcendent power and holiness. As

Creator, God maintains and sustains this creation, demonstrating God's immanent love and faithfulness. The rich diversity of life on earth, bound together in unity under God the Creator, was pronounced by God to be "very good" (Genesis 1:31). Thus "the earth is the Lord's, and everything in it" (Psalm 24:1); "everything God created is good, and nothing is to be rejected if it is received with thanksgiving" (1 Timothy 4:4).

Yet God's good creation has been corrupted by the power of sin. According to the Genesis narrative, the comprehensive verdict of "death" for human sin includes not just an accursed humanity but also an accursed creation (Genesis 3:17–19). Or, as Paul describes this in his letter to the Romans, "the creation was subjected to frustration, not by its own choice, but by the will of the one who subjected it"—it is now "groaning" in its "bondage to decay" because of human sin (Romans 8:20–22).

Thus a full renovation of God's good creation is needed, and the Old Testament prophetic writings reflect the ancient Israelite expectation of this eschatological renewal. This expectation of "new creation" was bound up with other prophetic hopes, especially those related to the Messiah and the kingdom of God. At the time when the Messianic son of David is revealed, bringing about God's saving sovereignty for the people of God, the earth would be returned to its Edenic peace: "The wolf will live with the lamb, the leopard will lie down with the goat, the calf and the lion and the yearling together; and a little child will lead them" (Isaiah 11:6). At the time when God's saving sovereignty is displayed, restoring God's people, all creation would be restored as well, bringing about a "new heavens and a new earth" which would endure forever (Isaiah 65:17; 66:22).

The resurrection of the crucified Jesus affirms these concepts and accomplishes these expectations. *By resurrecting the crucified Jesus, God has re-affirmed that his creation is very good.* The galaxies, the stars, the earth, life on earth—all this is not some cosmic accident, nor is it some divine mistake. This truth is affirmed throughout the Christian Scriptures in many ways, but it is decisively re-affirmed in Jesus' resurrection from the dead. As we discovered earlier, "resurrection" does not refer to some disembodied spiritual existence after death; rather, "resurrection" refers to a transformed bodily existence within space and time, a renewal of what was and not a replacement with something else entirely. By resurrecting the crucified Jesus from the dead, God has declared that he is not giving up on his sin-scarred creation, that the "very good" created order is instead to be redeemed and renovated. The earth is not some temporary shelter for humanity, to be discarded once it is worn out; rather, in spite of its "bondage to decay" it remains God's glorious handiwork, reflecting the transcendence and immanence, creative power and loving faithfulness of its Creator, and it must be guarded and treasured for this very purpose.

Moreover, *by resurrecting the crucified Jesus, God has begun the process of renewing the creation.* God the Creator became "enfleshed" or "incarnate" in Jesus the unique Son of God, fully participating in his good creation which had been corrupted by the sin of humanity. In his suffering and death Jesus fully embraced creation's corruption, immersing himself in the curse of sin and death. And by resurrecting the crucified Jesus from the dead, God began the divine program of creation renewal, transforming Jesus to a new existence untouched by the curse of sin and death. This creation renewal is an ongoing, present process, as God works to restore the good creation degraded by human sin. But ultimately this creation renewal will only be completed at the return of Jesus from heaven, when "the time comes for God to restore everything, as he promised long ago through his holy prophets" (Acts 3:21). Then there will be a "new heaven and a new earth, where righteousness dwells" (2 Peter 3:13), where "no longer will there be any curse" because "the old order of things has passed away" (Revelation 21:4; 22:3). Creation will finally be "liberated from its bondage to decay" (Romans 8:20–22); the restoration of God's good creation—God's reconciliation of all things in heaven and on earth (Colossians 1:20)—will be complete.

ॐ

As humanity is part of God's creation, the story of humanity is embedded within this larger story of creation and new creation. A recurring scene in our journey so far has been the creation of humanity in "the image of God," designed by God to be God's royal representatives on earth and to reflect God's character in relationship with him. Humanity was created to be God's vassal kings, extending and ensuring God's sovereign rule over the earth, a rule characterized not by oppressive conquest but by faithful care. Humanity was created to be God's children, demonstrating God's faithful and loving character in ongoing relationship with one another and with the Creator. But the curse of sin which has affected all creation has especially affected humanity, bringing hostility and oppression to human relationships, pain and futility to human existence, and the finality of death to human life.

However, as we have seen, God the Father—the origin of, authority over, and caregiver for all creation—longs for the return of his human creatures to their intended purpose in intimate relationship with him. Therefore God has acted to deliver humanity from the curse of sin and death through the crucified and resurrected Jesus. In the death of Jesus, sin is forgiven in atonement, paid for in redemption, forgotten in new covenant, challenged in cruciform suffering, and vanquished in paradoxical victory. In the resurrection of Jesus, death is reversed: its condemnation turns into justification, its shame into honor, its oppression into liberation, and all human futility, pain, hostility, and death is transformed into life and peace.

In the crucified and resurrected Jesus, then, God is creating a new humanity. Because of human disobedience, the first humanity was patterned after the tragic story of Adam, and thus is a humanity scarred by the curse of sin and death, hostility and futility. Paul describes this as being "in Adam," living within the sphere of human existence marked off by Adam's sin and death (Romans 5:12–21; 1 Corinthians 15:20–28, 42–49). But the new humanity is patterned after the story of Jesus; it is a humanity generated by the resurrection of the crucified Jesus. In contrast to being "in Adam," Paul describes this new humanity as being "in Christ," living within the sphere of human existence marked off by Christ's death and resurrection. As Paul declares, "if anyone is in Christ, the new creation has come" (2 Corinthians 5:17)—that person is part of God's new humanity in his program of creation renewal.

As we have already explored, this new humanity is being created in the image of Christ by the Spirit of Christ, a Christ-likeness which has a particular shape: the pattern of the crucified and resurrected Jesus. Thus, one way of describing this Christ-likeness which distinguishes the new humanity is with the triad of key words used by the earliest Christians to describe Jesus in his death and resurrection: *faith, hope, and love.* As we have seen, Jesus' faith was shown in his loyal dependence upon his loving and faithful Father to bring about his good purposes, even through his suffering and death on a cross. Jesus' hope was displayed in his confident expectation even in the midst of suffering that God would vindicate him through his resurrection. And Jesus' love was demonstrated in his complete self-giving for the benefit of others through his suffering and death.

As the new humanity "in Christ," being created in Christ-likeness by the Spirit of Christ, God's people are to be characterized by this faith, hope, and love of Jesus. In this light Christian *faith* is belief in the good news of salvation through the crucified and resurrected Jesus, trust in God the Father acting through his Son Jesus to bring about God's good purposes for creation, and loyal dependence upon the loving and faithful God patterned after Jesus' own relationship to the Father. Christian *hope* is confident expectation of divine renewal and vindication through resurrection, patterned after Jesus' attitude toward his own future and based upon Jesus' resurrection from the dead. And Christian *love* is a complete self-giving for the benefit of others, even for those viewed by the world as the last, the least, and the lost, patterned after Jesus' self-giving life, suffering, and death for sinners. All Christian ethics—whether personal morality or social action—is bound up in these three virtues which stem from the life, teachings, death, and resurrection of Jesus. "But the greatest of these is love," Paul says (1 Corinthians

13:13), for "love is the fulfillment of the Law," the fulfillment of all God's eternal purposes of humanity (Romans 13:10), an idea which echoes the traditional teaching of Jesus (Matthew 22:37–40). Or, as 1 John states, "let us love one another, for love comes from God. Everyone who loves has been born of God and knows God. Whoever does not love does not know God, because God is love" (1 John 4:7–8).

Like the new creation of which it is a part, this new humanity will not be fully restored until Jesus appears again. In the resurrection of the crucified Jesus God's creation renewal program has begun, God's new cross-and-resurrection-patterned humanity has been initiated. But it will not be until Jesus returns from heaven that "the creation itself will be liberated from its bondage to decay and brought into the freedom and glory of the children of God," humanity's full "adoption, the redemption of our bodies" (Romans 8:18–23). Then God's people will be fully "conformed to the image of his Son" or "glorified," which is the very purpose of God for humanity (Romans 8:28–30). At Christ's return those who are "in Christ" will be resurrected to the same transformed existence as Jesus, fully participating in God's renewal and vindication, forever untouched by sin and death: at his return "the Lord Jesus Christ . . . will transform our lowly bodies so that they will be like his glorious body" (Philippians 3:20–21); "when Christ appears, we shall be like him, for we shall see him as he is" (1 John 3:2). In this eternal new age, "There will be no more death or mourning or crying or pain, for the old order of things has passed away" (Revelation 21:4). God will have finally and decisively reclaimed his sovereignty over the creation, and the new humanity in God's image, the image of his Son, will extend God's loving, faithful rule over the new creation. In the language of Revelation, recalling the *imago Dei* language of Genesis, "they will reign for ever and ever" (Revelation 22:5).

CR

The reality of God's judgment of humanity for human sin is a constant theme through Scripture, and this theme gains momentum with a future dimension as one moves through the biblical writings. Scripture repeats this rather ominous refrain: God will one day pronounce judgment on every human being for his or her thoughts, words, and actions in this life (Ecclesiastes 12:14; Matthew 25:31–46; Romans 14:10–12; Revelation 20:11–15).

While much could be said about the diverse biblical conceptions of a future, final judgment, at the very least this reality must be placed within the setting of some landscapes we have explored thus far, especially God's love and justice as revealed in Jesus' death "for our sins" and Jesus' resurrection "on the third day." God's verdict on human sin has already taken place on the cross: sin is the scourge of humanity, its dark bane, needing the death of the incarnate God to deal with it decisively. And God has indeed dealt with sin through Jesus' death on the cross, so that those who participate in Jesus' death are guaranteed the bright blessing of the restored creation through Jesus' resurrection. Likewise, God's vindication of his people—even the entire created order being made right—has already happened through Jesus' resurrection from the dead, and those who participate in Jesus' resurrection will also take part in his vindication and renewal. Thus these threads of God's sin-defeating love and God's right-making justice run through to Christ's future return, where they are woven together in God's final judgment of humanity: the power of sin and death finally vanquished, the inequities of human history reversed, all creation made right again, God's new humanity restored in Christ-like glory.

◌੪

This new humanity is a collective concept: while individual persons are restored in the image of God in Christ, they are restored to relationship with God and others. To put this in Paul's terms, being "in Christ," or living in the sphere of existence marked off by Christ's death and resurrection, means that one is vitally connected with all others who are "in Christ." Or, to extend this language further, as Paul does, to be "in Christ" means that one is necessarily part of the "body of Christ": Christ is the head of this body, sustaining and controlling it, and believers in Christ are different parts of this body, doing Christ's will in the world (1 Corinthians 12; Ephesians 4:1–16). This new humanity is also described by more than one New Testament author as a temple for the purpose of worshipping God, with individual Christians like stones fitted together by God to build this sacred sanctuary of worship: God's people together contemplating God's character, remembering God's actions, hearing God's voice in Scripture and through his people, and responding in prayer, confession, thanksgiving, praise, and service (e.g., Ephesians 2:11–22; 1 Peter 2:4–10). But the most common image used in the New Testament for God's new humanity is that of an assembly of citizens, a "church" (*ekklēsia*). This term was taken up by the earliest Christians from the Old Greek version of the Jewish Scriptures, the Septuagint, where the term was used to refer to the ancient Israelites as the gathered people of

God. The church, then, is the new people of God, gathered in worship of God as God's temple, gathered to do God's will as Christ's body, marked off as God's new humanity by the Spirit of the crucified and resurrected Jesus.

The church has been given a particular task—"God's will as Christ's body"—in this time between Jesus' resurrection and his return, a task which grows out of the resurrection of the crucified Jesus. Proclaiming and living out the death and resurrection of Jesus in faith, hope, and love, as described above, the church is called to enact God's program of creation renewal in this age in anticipation of the fulfillment of the renewal of creation in the age to come. Another way to look at this task of creation renewal is to see it as simply fulfilling the purpose of humanity in the image of God, ensuring and extending God's loving and faithful rule throughout the earthly creation. Yet another way to see this creation renewal task is to understand it as applying the resurrection reversal of the crucified Jesus to the world around us. In Jesus' resurrection, condemnation, shame, oppression, and death have been transformed into vindication, glory, freedom, and life. Thus, by the Spirit of Jesus the church is called to bring restorative care to the earth, liberating justice to the oppressed, food to the hungry, comfort to the suffering, healing to the sick, forgiveness and honor to the guilty and shamed, love to those in need, faith to those who doubt, hope to those in despair—light and life to a dark and dying world. This resurrection reversal is both our salvation blessing and our missionary task.

Thus, God's new humanity is fully defined by the crucifixion and resurrection of Jesus. In this present age God's people are conformed to the suffering and crucifixion of

Jesus, shaped into his God-dependent faith, self-giving love, and resurrection-pointing hope. And God's people are called to bring the resurrection and exaltation of Jesus to others in this present age, bringing about creation renewal and resurrection reversal in the world by the power of the Spirit and in anticipation of Christ's return and the age to come. God's people are conformed to the death of Jesus in order to bring the life of Jesus to the world around them; or, in Paul's words, "We always carry around in our body the death of Jesus, so that the life of Jesus may also be revealed in our body. For we who are alive are always being given over to death for Jesus' sake, so that his life may be revealed in our mortal body. So then, death is at work in us, but life is at work in you" (2 Corinthians 4:10–12).

଼ଷ

Just as God's wider creation is characterized by "diversity-in-unity," so God's collective new humanity is also characterized by "diversity-in-unity." This should come as no surprise, since God himself is "three-in-one": the one God who is Father, Son, and Spirit, has fashioned a creation which reflects his own "diversity-in-unity," and his new creation and new humanity likewise reflect both unity and diversity (see 1 Corinthians 12:4–7; Ephesians 4:4–7). United by the Spirit of Christ and marked off by the crucifixion and resurrection of Christ, the new people of God are diverse in ethnicity, social status, and gender: "There is neither Jew nor Gentile, neither slave nor free, neither male nor female, for you are all one in Christ Jesus" (Galatians 3:28). While believers continue to be distinguishable as "Greek" or "free" or "female," these sorts of ethnic, social, and gender markers are irrelevant for determining one's status within the new humanity. Instead they contribute to a kaleidoscope of rich diversity within the one people of God.

Such diversity-in-unity is even to be found in the theology and practice of the people of God. We have seen this already in the New Testament interpretation and expression of the gospel of Jesus crucified and risen: while there were distinctive gospel messages each "according to" individual apostles, all these were expressions of the one "gospel."

A very illuminating example of this early Christian diversity-in-unity in theology and practice is found in Paul's letter to the Romans. Toward the end of this letter Paul turns to a dispute between "weak" and "strong" Christians in Rome (14:1—15:13). While it is not clear exactly what was going on in the Roman church, it seems likely that this was a dispute between a predominantly Jewish group and a predominantly Gentile group over specific religiously significant foods and holidays. The Jewish group was "weak in faith," that is, their consciences would not allow them to eat any food apart from that prescribed by the Jewish Law, nor could they in good conscience refrain from observing the Sabbath as prescribed by the Law. The Gentile group, however, was "strong in faith," that is, their consciences were not constrained by the Jewish Law and so they could eat any food they wished and treat every day alike. At least from the perspective of the "weak in faith," this was a very significant issue; and for both groups, this was an issue that was addressed to some extent by their shared Scriptures, in the laws of Moses regarding sacred days and ritually pure foods.

Paul's response is telling. He does not argue from Scripture, that the food and Sabbath laws are commanded by God in the Bible and therefore must be kept by everyone. Nor does he argue from significance, that this is an important issue and so all must come to a uniform consensus. It would seem that, for Paul, *a belief or practice could be both significant and biblically grounded—and yet not be an essential Christian belief or practice.* Rather, Paul argues for diversity-in-unity on the basis of the death and resurrection of Jesus: the crucified and resurrected Jesus is Lord over both Jewish and Gentile believers, so each one must act according to his or her conscience before the Lord (14:4–12); through the crucified and resurrected Jesus God has accepted both Jewish and Gentile believers, so each group must likewise accept the other (14:1–3; 15:1–13); and ultimately, the kingdom of God brought about by the crucified and resurrected Jesus "is not a matter of eating and drinking, but of righteousness, peace and joy in the Holy Spirit" (14:17). In other words, the Roman Christians were to be unified in the crucified and risen Jesus by his Spirit under God, even as they could display an acceptable diversity in more secondary, if still significant, religious beliefs and practices.

So what exactly is the center of authentic Christian faith and life which should unify Christians? This is no small question, but the example of Romans 14–15 underscores an answer we have seen throughout our journey: the resurrection of the crucified Jesus is the ground and center of all truly Christian thought and action, both the source and the focus of all belief and behavior that can be called authentically Christian. The following diagram might be helpful for conceptualizing this center, as well as the theological and practical diversity-in-unity which flows from it:

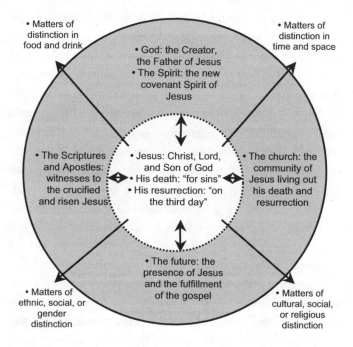

The center circle of the diagram represents the core elements of the gospel, the ground and center of essential Christian faith and life: Jesus and his salvific death and resurrection. This is the irreducible minimum of authentic Christian faith and life. That is, genuine Christianity is all about knowing and following the crucified and resurrected Jesus, living out his salvific death and resurrection in faith, love, and hope. The second circle represents those beliefs and practices which directly grow out of the reality of the resurrection of the crucified Jesus, even as they in turn impact one's understanding and experience of the crucified and resurrected Jesus—thus the two-way arrows between these circles. Together, these two circles are the absolute essentials of historically orthodox Christian theology and practice. That is, historically orthodox Christianity is focused on the salvific work of the triune God through the crucified and resurrected Jesus, as witnessed by the Scriptures, proclaimed and lived out by the church, and fulfilled in the future eschaton. Most prominently, this focus can be seen in formal historic Christian creeds such as the Apostles' Creed and the Nicene Creed, each with a Trinitarian structure centered on the gospel story of Jesus' suffering, death, resurrection, and exaltation.

Beyond these circles are matters which may hold a high degree of significance for certain Christians or Christian communities, matters which may even be perceived to have solid biblical support, but which nevertheless are not central to authentic or orthodox Christianity. As the diagram shows, I would suggest that these sorts of matters can be categorized around four related poles: matters of food and drink, in which people create distinctions between persons or groups based on in their attitude toward certain foods or drinks; matters of time and space, in which similar distinctions are made in terms of special days or places; matters of ethnic, social, or gender distinction, distinguishing persons or groups on the basis of these realities; and matters in which similar distinctions are made on the basis of cultural, social, or religious factors. As is illustrated by the example of Romans 14–15 discussed above—and represented in other New Testament texts as well—these are the sorts of issues which the early Christians highlighted as secondary issues or matters of personal conscience, matters for which one can expect to find a legitimate diversity. The consumption of alcohol, the restriction of Sunday activities, the structure of the local church, the

style and form of corporate worship, the role of women in
ministry, the practice of tithing, the mode of baptism—these
and many others are among the potentially divisive issues
which are secondary matters that sit within the realm of legitimate diversity. These matters are always to be informed by
the center—indeed, they should be radically *transformed* by
the gospel of the crucified and risen Jesus—thus the arrows
in the diagram outward from the center circle. Nevertheless,
these matters, while significant in particular situations and
even having claims of biblical backing for alternative view-
points, are neither the center nor its most immediate implications. In other words, no particular view on these matters is
essential to authentic and orthodox Christianity.

One important qualification must be made: while the
central matters within the two circles are more complex than
is represented in this simple diagram, not all further implications of these matters are as central as others. For example,
God the Creator is central to orthodox Christianity, but not
any particular belief about the means and timing of creation;
the future return of Christ is central, but not any particular
view of when and how this will happen; the church is central, but not any particular stance on church governance or
ordinances; the Scriptures are central, but not any particular
theory of Scripture's inspiration; the presence and work of the
Spirit is central, but not any particular notion of sanctification; the salvific significance of Jesus' death is central, but no
particular theory of atonement is exclusively so; and so on.
These sorts of specific beliefs, while not insignificant, are not
essential. They may in fact be further examples of the more
peripheral matters noted above. This means that while they
may hold a high degree of significance for certain Christians

or Christian communities and they may even be perceived to have solid biblical support, they are nevertheless not essential to authentic or orthodox Christianity. Moreover, these sorts of particular beliefs simply illustrate the reality we have already seen in the apostolic unity and diversity related to the gospel, that the resurrection of the crucified Jesus is the source of both genuine Christian unity and acceptable Christian diversity.

However we conceive of acceptable diversity and necessary unity within Christian theology and practice, it would seem that the Christian Scriptures allow for greater diversity than some Christians are comfortable with while also calling for a more fundamental unity than others might like. This could well be stated even more strongly: God—whose eternal being and creative activity both reflect diversity-in-unity—rejoices in the diversity-in-unity of the new humanity generated by the resurrection of the crucified Jesus. God delights in the diversity of believers in the one gospel who come from all social and ethnic backgrounds, and God glories in the diversity of expressions of the one church's faith, hope, and love.

❧

In the beginning God raised Jesus from the dead.

For Christians, Jesus' resurrection from the dead was a new beginning, the vindication of our Messiah and our Lord, the Son of God. Jesus' resurrection was the end of his predetermined end, the beginning of a promised new existence. For Christians, Jesus' resurrection from the dead was a fresh start in God's action in the world, even the beginning of a new act of creation. By raising Jesus from the dead, transforming him to a new life untouched by sin and death, God initiated a new era in the history of humanity and the world.

This event is also the beginning of a new way of thinking for Christians, a new way of perceiving reality and knowing truth. The resurrection of Jesus was, in the sharpest sense of the term, an "apocalyptic" event; that is, it turned the world upside down and so changed forever the way in which the world must be viewed. Indeed, the resurrection of the crucified Jesus is the ground and center of all truly Christian thought and action, both the source and the focus of all belief and behavior that can be called authentically Christian. All distinctively Christian theology and practice should grow out of the reality—and be centered on the reality—that the crucified Jesus has been resurrected from the dead. In other words, the resurrection of the crucified Jesus is both the starting place and the compass for Christians in our journey to understand God and God's work in the world and to live out God's purposes for us.

It is a journey well worth making, with vast new vistas yet to be explored.

After reading . . .

- In what ways should Jesus' death and resurrection impact our perspective on the created world around us?

- What does it mean to say that "in the crucified and resurrected Jesus, God is creating a new humanity"? What is this "new humanity"? What identifying marks distinguish this "new humanity"? What is the purpose of this "new humanity"?

- What will be accomplished for creation and humanity when Jesus returns?

- What does it mean to say that God's people should be characterized by "diversity-in-unity"? Theologically and practically, what is the essential core of authentic Christianity? What do you think of this perspective on "diversity-in-unity"? How might this be worked out in your local church?

- What are some of the "vast new vistas" in theology Christians must explore today? What about questions stemming from religious pluralism, or issues of social justice or morality, or environmental concerns? How might the resurrection of the crucified Jesus be both "the starting place and the compass" in exploring an appropriate Christian theology and practice related to these issues?

For further reading . . .

BIBLICAL TEXTS:
Genesis 1–3; Isaiah 11, 65–66; Acts 2; Romans 5, 8, 14–15; 1 Corinthians 12–13, 15; Ephesians 4; 1 Thessalonians 4–5; 1 Peter 2; 2 Peter 3; Revelation 21–22.

Gorman, Michael J. *Cruciformity: Paul's Narrative Spirituality of the Cross.* Grand Rapids: Eerdmans, 2001.

An exploration of Paul's distinctive emphasis on Jesus' self-giving, life-giving death as a pattern for Christian life, ministry, and ethics.

Hays, Richard B. *The Moral Vision of the New Testament: Community, Cross, New Creation: A Contemporary Introduction to New Testament Ethics.* San Francisco: HarperSanFrancisco, 1996.

A thorough, scholarly discussion of the way in which the story of the crucified and resurrected Jesus shaped the ethical teaching of the New Testament, and the significance of this for Christian ethics today.

Moltmann, Jürgen. *The Coming of God: Christian Eschatology.* Minneapolis: Fortress, 1996.

A scholarly exploration of the Christian doctrine of eschatology, including the nature and significance of the future resurrection, the return of Christ, and the "new creation."

Pannenberg, Wolfhart. *Anthropology in Theological Perspective.* Translated by Matthew J. O'Connell. Edinburgh: T. & T. Clark, 1999.

A scholarly exploration of the Christian doctrine of anthropology, including the significance of Jesus human nature, death, and resurrection for understanding the nature and purpose of humanity.

Wright, N. T. *Surprised by Hope: Rethinking Heaven, the Resurrection, and the Mission of the Church.* New York: HarperOne, 2008.

An accessible study of the significance of the resurrection for Christian theology and practice, particularly in terms of eschatology and ecclesiology.

For further reading in general Christian theology . . .

Marshall, I. Howard. *New Testament Theology: Many Witnesses, One Gospel.* Downers Grove, IL: InterVarsity Press, 2004.

A thorough exploration of the theological perspectives of the New Testament, centered on the gospel of Jesus Christ.

McGrath, Alister E. *Christian Theology: An Introduction.* 4th ed. Oxford: Blackwell, 2007.

A thorough, general introduction to Christian theology.

Migliore, Daniel L. *Faith Seeking Understanding: An Introduction to Christian Theology.* 2nd ed. Grand Rapids: Eerdmans, 2004.

A general introduction to Christian theology.

Schlatter, Adolf. *The Theology of the Apostles: The Development of New Testament Theology.* Translated by Andreas J. Köstenberger. 2nd ed. Grand Rapids: Baker, 1999.

A classic treatment of the theological perspectives of Jesus and the earliest Christians.

Thielman, Frank. *Theology of the New Testament: A Canonical and Synthetic Approach.* Grand Rapids: Zondervan, 2005.

An exploration of the theological perspectives of the New Testament, centered on the grace of God shown in Jesus.

Williams, Rowan. *Tokens of Trust: An Introduction to Christian Belief.* Louisville: Westminster John Knox Press, 2007.

An accessible introduction to Christian theology focused on the Apostles' Creed.

Wright, N. T. *Simply Christian: Why Christianity Makes Sense.* San Francisco: HarperSanFrancisco, 2006.

An accessible introduction to Christian theology and practice emphasizing the coherence of a Christian worldview with the human experience.

Epilogue

The Apostles' Creed

FOR NEARLY TWO thousand years Christians have witnessed to the resurrection of the crucified Jesus, centering their faith and life on the good news of salvation through Christ.

The early Church Fathers, Christian leaders after the time of the Jesus and the apostles, summarized these essential matters of Christian faith and life in what came to be known as the "rule of faith," outlined in a threefold structure focused on Father, Son, and Spirit, with the crucial narrative about Christ in the center. This gospel-centered and Trinitarian-structured summary of belief eventually became formalized in what is known as the Apostles' Creed, one of the great symbols of the Christian faith to this day:

> We believe in God, the Father almighty, creator of
> heaven and earth.
>
> We believe in Jesus Christ, God's only Son, our
> Lord,
> who was conceived by the Holy Spirit,
> born of the virgin Mary,
> suffered under Pontius Pilate,

was crucified, died, and was buried;
he descended to the dead.
On the third day he rose again;
he ascended into heaven,
he is seated at the right hand of the Father,
and he will come to judge the living and the
dead.

We believe in the Holy Spirit,
the holy catholic church,
the communion of saints,
the forgiveness of sins,
the resurrection of the body,
and the life everlasting. Amen.

Glossary

Abba. Aramaic, "father." Used by Jesus and the early Christians in reference to God, indicating both familial intimacy and submissive respect.

AD. Latin *Anno Domini*, "in the year of our Lord," designating the years since the birth of Jesus according to an early medieval calculation. Alternatively CE ("Common Era"), used in sensitivity to non-Christian historians and a religiously pluralist society.

anthropology, anthropological. From Greek *anthrōpos*, "humanity," and *logia*, "rational discourse." The doctrine of or teaching about the nature and purpose of humanity.

apocalypse, apocalyptic. From Greek *apokalypsis*, "revelation," originating from the opening self-reference in Revelation 1:1. As a noun, an ancient genre of writing often characterized by visions of bizarre imagery interpreted by angelic guides and purporting to provide a prophetic glimpse of future events culminating in the dramatic eschatological intervention of God into human history, overthrowing present evil powers; as an adjective, referring to any writing or concept related to the characteristics of an apocalypse.

apostle, apostolic. From Greek *apostolos*, "envoy." Any person sent as a representative of the sender or sending group, e.g., a specific church; in a special sense of those people singled out by Christ to be his authoritative representatives and spokespersons, sometimes "Apostle."

atonement, atoning. An act which restores the relationship, broken by sin, between God and humans.

baptism, baptismal. A ritual using water, often through full immersion, which initiates the person into a religious community and/or is performed in relation to the forgiveness of their sins.

BC. "Before Christ," designating the years before the birth of Jesus according to an early medieval calculation. Alternatively BCE ("Before Common Era"), used in sensitivity to non-Christian historians and a religiously pluralist society.

Bible, biblical. From Greek *biblion*, "scroll, book." Canonical writings collected together, often in a single binding. The Christian Bible consists of the Old and New Testaments. Also "Scripture," "the Scriptures."

bibliology, bibliological. From Greek *biblion*, "scroll, book," and *logia*, "rational discourse." The doctrine of or teaching about the nature and purpose of the Bible.

canon, canonical. From Greek *kanōn*, "rule, measuring stick." A collection of documents which are authoritative for the belief and practice of a religious community; specifically, the collection of documents in the Christian Bible.

Christ. From Greek *christos*, "anointed one." The mediator of eschatological deliverance anticipated by much of early Judaism, most often understood as a king in the dynastic line of David. The Greek term "Christ" became used almost exclusively by early Christians in reference to Jesus, while the Hebrew/Aramaic term "Messiah" could be used to refer to anyone thought to be this deliverer.

Christianity, Christian. The religion and way of life of professing followers of Jesus, in the first century AD centered on Jesus as founding teacher, miracle-worker, and prophet, and crucified, risen, and exalted Messiah, Lord, and Son of God.

Christology, christological. From Greek *christos*, "anointed one," and *logia*, "rational discourse." The doctrine of or teaching about the person and work of Jesus Christ.

church. The universal community of Christians; more often, any specific local assembly of Christians. See also **ecclesiology**.

covenant. A formal agreement between two parties outlining the responsibilities and privileges of their relationship. Common biblical covenants include: the covenant God established with Abraham and his descendants (Genesis 15, 17); with the ancient nation of Israel through Moses at Mount Sinai (Exodus 19–24); the "new covenant" promised through the Old Testament prophets (e.g., Jeremiah 31).

creed, creedal. A statement of religious belief, often in a memorable, formulaic arrangement.

crucifixion, crucified. A form of ancient execution practiced by the Romans in the first century AD, involving the suspension of a live person from a cross of vertical and horizontal beams until the person died, normally of asphyxiation.

ecclesiology, ecclesiological. From Greek *ekklēsia*, "gathering, assembly," and *logia*, "rational discourse." The doctrine of or teaching about the nature and purpose of the church.

eschatology, eschatological. From Greek *eschatos*, "last (thing)," and *logia*, "rational discourse." The doctrine of or teaching about the future, or specifically on the end of the present world order or state of affairs. See also **eschaton**.

eschaton. From Greek *eschatos*, "last (thing)." The end of the present world order and the creation of a new world order or state of affairs. See also **eschatology**.

Eucharist, eucharistic. A Christian ritual meal related to the Jewish Passover, focused on eating bread as the broken body of Jesus and drinking wine as the shed blood of Jesus, in memory of Jesus' salvific death.

faith. Adherence to and/or dependence upon a person or idea; specifically often adherence to Christian teaching and/or dependence upon God. Greek *pistis*.

Gentile. Used from a Jewish perspective to refer to a non-Jewish person.

god/goddess, God. A divine being, normally "god/goddess"; specifically in Christianity and Judaism, the only existing divine being who created all things, normally "God."

gospel, Gospel. The Christian message of salvation about Jesus crucified and resurrected, or the historical events underlying this theological interpretation, often as "gospel"; or, in later usage, any ancient collection of traditions about Jesus, whether in narrative, thematic, or formal arrangement, often as "Gospel."

Greco-Roman. Pertaining to the mixed Greek and Roman culture of much of the Mediterranean region in the first century AD.

halakah, halakic. Hebrew, "to walk." Rulings or interpretations on specific points of the Jewish Law. Also "*halakha*," "*halakhah*," "*halacha*."

hamartiology, hamartiological. From Greek *hamartia*, "sin," and *logia*, "rational discourse." The doctrine of or teaching about the origin and nature of sin.

history, historical. Events that have happened in the past; or writing about past events; or the discipline which studies past events.

holiness, holy. The quality or state of being set apart, distinct from other entities, in terms of identity and/or behavior; specifically, God's "complete otherness" in relation to creation. See also **sanctification**.

hope. Confident expectation of a future good; specifically often confident expectation of future renewal and vindication by God at the resurrection. Greek *elpis*.

imago Dei. Latin, "image of God." Refers to the creation of humanity in the "image of God" as described in Genesis 1, involving humanity's representation of God's kingship over the earth and reflection of God's character in relationship with him.

immanence, immanent. God's manifestation within time and space, God's "intimate nearness" in relation to creation.

incarnation, incarnate. God becoming human or "enfleshed" in Jesus (John 1:14).

inspiration, inspired. The Bible's production under divine influence. Translated from Greek *theopneustos*, "God-breathed," in 2 Timothy 3:16.

Jesus. Jesus of Nazareth (ca. 6 BC—AD 30), a Jewish teacher, miracle-worker, and prophet who became the originator of Christianity and object of Christian devotion.

Jew, Jewish. A physical descendant of the patriarch Jacob (Israel) and/or a full adherent of Judaism; pertaining to Judaism.

Jewish Scriptures. The Bible of Judaism, identical in content (but not order) to the Christian Old Testament, consisting of mostly Hebrew writings from roughly the 10th to the 3rd centuries BC. Also "Hebrew Bible," "Tanak," "Tanakh."

John, Johannine. John son of Zebedee (d. ca. AD 95), one of the original Jewish disciples of Jesus who became a significant leader in the early Christian movement.

Judaism, Judaic. The religion and way of life of the Jewish people, in the first century AD centered on monotheism, belief in their divine election as a nation, observance of the Law (especially Sabbath-keeping, male circumcision, and ritual purity regulations), and temple worship.

justification, justify. The present divine consideration of a person as righteous on the basis of the atonement of Christ in his crucifixion; or the ongoing process of being made righteous in practice on the same basis; or the future vindication of God's people at the eschaton on the same basis. Combinations or other nuances of these may be possible. Greek *dikaioō*.

kingdom of God. God's eschatological deliverance of the people of God and sovereignty over the earth; in Jewish expectation in the first century AD, often thought to arrive through a messiah.

Law. The Jewish Scriptures, in whole or part (i.e. the first five books of Moses); or the Law given through Moses, the legal commandments given in the Mosaic covenant. Other nuances of these may be discernible as well. Also "Torah."

Lord. A (divine) master. Greek *kyrios*.

Lord's Supper. See **Eucharist**.

love. Personal affection for others and/or selfless action for the benefit of others; specifically often God's selfless action in Christ's death on the cross for the benefit of humanity, or Christians' selfless action for the benefit of others. Greek *agapē*, *philia*.

Messiah, messiah, messianic. From Hebrew *mashiah*, "anointed one." See **Christ**.

millennialism, millenarianism. From Latin *millennium*, "thousand years," originating in reference to the "one thousand year" reign of Christ in Revelation 20:4–6. Any belief in such a reign of Christ; or more generally, any belief in a future "golden age" of humanity, often in contrast to a present era perceived as evil or flawed in some way.

narrative. A written or oral account of events in the form and style of a story.

New Testament. The distinctively Christian writings of the Christian Bible, consisting of twenty-seven first-century AD documents originally written in Greek: Matthew, Mark, Luke, John, Acts, Romans, 1–2 Corinthians, Galatians, Ephesians, Philippians, Colossians, 1–2 Thessalonians, 1–2 Timothy, Titus, Philemon, Hebrews, James, 1–2 Peter, 1–3 John, Jude, and Revelation. Abbreviated "NT."

Old Testament. From the perspective of Christianity, the "pre-Christian" writings of the Christian Bible. Abbreviated "OT." See **Jewish Scriptures**.

omnipotence, omnipotent. God's sovereign power to do whatever God wills to do.

omnipresence, omnipresent. God's personal presence in all places and times.

omniscience, omniscient. God's total perception of all things in all times and places, and God's complete knowledge of all things in all times and places.

oral tradition. Traditions passed on to successive generations by word of mouth; specifically, such traditions in early Christianity related to Jesus' life, teachings, death, and resurrection.

Passover. The annual Jewish memorial festival which celebrates the deliverance of the ancient Israelites from Egypt under Moses.

Paul, Pauline. Paul of Tarsus (d. ca. AD 66), also called Saul, a Pharisaic Jew who became a follower of Jesus after a visionary experience in which he believed he saw the resurrected Jesus.

Pentecost. An annual Jewish barley harvest festival fifty days after Passover; or specifically, as described in Acts 2, the Pentecost during which the Spirit came in power upon Jesus' disciples, giving them courage for witnessing to Jesus' death and resurrection.

Peter, Petrine. Simon Peter (d. ca. AD 66), one of the original Jewish disciples of Jesus who became a significant leader in the early Christian movement.

Pharisee, Pharisaic. A voluntary group in early Judaism which sought to interpret and live out the Law in all areas of life according to a particular set of oral traditions.

pneumatology, pneumatological. From Greek *pneuma*, "spirit," and *logia*, "rational discourse." The doctrine of or teaching about the person and work of the Holy Spirit.

reconciliation The bringing together of two previously hostile parties; specifically, the bringing together of God and sinful humanity, and humans to one another, through Christ.

redemption, redemptive. Deliverance from oppression or emancipation from slavery; specifically, deliverance and emancipation from sin through Christ.

resurrection, resurrected (risen). The return to bodily life after being dead; or more technically, such a return to bodily life in a transformed existence, believed in much of first-century AD Judaism and Christianity to happen at the eschaton.

righteousness, righteous. The condition of being and/or living as one should within the context of a covenant relationship. Greek *dikaiosynē*, *dikaios*. See also **justification**.

salvation, salvific. Divine rescue from sin and/or its associated results or effects; sometimes also related to deliverance from political or social oppression. Greek *sōtēria*.

sanctification, sanctified. Being set apart for God, either through ritual purity for temple worship, or from sin for salvation and service. See also **holiness**.

Savior. One who brings salvation. Greek *sōtēr*.

Scripture, scriptural. From Latin, *scriptura*, "writing." See **Bible**.

Septuagint, Septuagintal. The ancient Greek translation of the Jewish Scriptures, completed in Alexandria, Egypt, between roughly 300 and 100 BC. Abbreviated LXX. Also "Old Greek version."

shalom. Hebrew, "peace, wholeness, harmony." Refers to a blessed existence within creation in relationship with God.

sin. A trespass of divine law and/or a deviation from the divinely ordained moral order; more generally, a principle or power at work in humanity which results in such trespasses or deviations.

Son of God. A messianic title used in reference to the kings in the line of David; or, a title of divinity for Jesus implying an ontological relationship with God the Father.

soteriology, soteriological. From Greek *sōtēria*, "salvation, deliverance," and *logia*, "rational discourse." The doctrine of or teaching about the basis and nature of salvation.

spirit, Spirit. The non-material aspect of a human being; or a personal, non-material being; or the non-material, personal, powerful presence of God, normally "Spirit" or "Holy Spirit."

theology, theological. From Greek *theos*, "God," and *logia*, "rational discourse." The doctrine of or teaching about the nature, person, and work of God, or more generally about the totality of one's religious beliefs; or, the discipline which studies God and/or religious beliefs.

Torah. Hebrew, "law, life instruction." See **Law**.

tradition, traditions. Community instruction which is intended to be transmitted across successive generations or geographical distance, and thus is normally transmitted in a formal or even formulaic way; specifically, such traditions in early Christianity related to Jesus' life, teachings, death, and resurrection.

transcendence, transcendent. God's existence outside time and space, his "utter beyondness" in relation to creation.

Trinity, trinitarian. The Christian doctrine of God's "tri-unity," that God is one God in three distinct persons: Father, Son, and Holy Spirit.

YHWH. The name of the one true God in the Hebrew Bible. Derived from the Hebrew for "I am," as described in Exodus 3. Also "Yahweh"; sometimes "Jehovah."

Bibliography

Bauckham, Richard. *Jesus and the God of Israel: God Crucified and Other Studies on the New Testament's Christology of Divine Identity*. Grand Rapids: Eerdmans, 2008.

Bird, Michael F. *Are You the One Who Is to Come? The Historical Jesus and the Messianic Question*. Grand Rapids: Baker, 2009.

Carroll, John T., and Joel B. Green. *The Death of Jesus in Early Christianity*. Peabody, MA: Hendrickson, 1995.

Dunn, James D. G. *Jesus and the Spirit: A Study of the Religious and Charismatic Experience of Jesus and the First Christians as Reflected in the New Testament*. Philadelphia: Westminster, 1975.

———. *Jesus Remembered*. Christianity in the Making 1. Grand Rapids: Eerdmans, 2003.

Fee, Gordon D. *God's Empowering Presence: The Holy Spirit in the Letters of Paul*. Peabody, MA: Hendrickson, 1994.

———. *Paul, the Spirit, and the People of God*. Peabody, MA: Hendrickson, 1996.

———. *Pauline Christology: An Exegetical-Theological Study*. Peabody, MA: Hendrickson, 2007.

Gorman, Michael J. *Cruciformity: Paul's Narrative Spirituality of the Cross*. Grand Rapids: Eerdmans, 2001.

Green, Joel B., and Mark D. Baker. *Recovering the Scandal of the Cross: Atonement in New Testament & Contemporary Contexts*. Downers Grove, IL: InterVarsity, 2000.

Hays, Richard B. *The Moral Vision of the New Testament: Community, Cross, New Creation: A Contemporary Introduction to New Testament Ethics*. San Francisco: HarperSanFrancisco, 1996.

Hengel, Martin. *Crucifixion in the Ancient World and the Folly of the Message of the Cross*. Philadelphia: Fortress, 1977.

———. *The Four Gospels and the One Gospel of Jesus Christ: An Investigation of the Collection and Origin of the Canonical Gospels*. London: SCM, 2000.

Hurtado, Larry W. *How on Earth Did Jesus Become a God? Historical Questions about Earliest Devotion to Jesus*. Grand Rapids: Eerdmans, 2005.

———. *Lord Jesus Christ: Devotion to Jesus in Earliest Christianity*. Grand Rapids: Eerdmans, 2003.

Jervis, L. Ann. *At the Heart of the Gospel: Suffering in the Earliest Christian Message*. Grand Rapids: Eerdmans, 2007.

Kirk, J. R. Daniel. *Unlocking Romans: Resurrection and the Justification of God*. Grand Rapids: Eerdmans, 2008.

Ladd, George Eldon. *A Theology of the New Testament*. Rev. ed. Grand Rapids: Eerdmans, 1993.

Longenecker, Richard N., editor. *Life in the Face of Death: The Resurrection Message of the New Testament*. McMaster New Testament Studies. Grand Rapids: Eerdmans, 1998.

Madigan, Kevin J., and Jon D. Levenson. *Resurrection: The Power of God for Christians and Jews*. New Haven, CT: Yale University Press, 2008.

Marshall, I. Howard. *New Testament Theology: Many Witnesses, One Gospel*. Downers Grove, IL: InterVarsity, 2004.

McGrath, Alister E. *Christian Theology: An Introduction*. 4th ed. Oxford: Blackwell, 2007.

McKnight, Scot. *A Community Called Atonement*. Living Theology. Nashville, TN: Abingdon, 2007.

———. *Jesus and His Death: Historiography, the Historical Jesus, and Atonement Theory*. Waco, TX: Baylor University Press, 2005.

———. *The Jesus Creed: Loving God, Loving Others*. Brewster, MA: Paraclete, 2004.

Migliore, Daniel L. *Faith Seeking Understanding: An Introduction to Christian Theology*. 2nd ed. Grand Rapids: Eerdmans, 2004.

Moltmann, Jürgen. *The Coming of God: Christian Eschatology*. Minneapolis: Fortress, 1996.

———. *The Crucified God: The Cross of Christ as the Foundation and Criticism of Christian Theology*. London: SCM Press, 1974.

Neufeld, Thomas R. Yoder. *Recovering Jesus: The Witness of the New Testament.* Grand Rapids: Brazos, 2007.

Pannenberg, Wolfhart. *Anthropology in Theological Perspective.* Translated by Matthew J. O'Connell. Edinburgh: T. & T. Clark, 1999.

———. *Jesus, God and Man.* Translated by Lewis L. Wilkins and Duane A. Priebe. 2nd ed. Philadelphia: Westminster, 1977.

Schlatter, Adolf. *The Theology of the Apostles: The Development of New Testament Theology.* Translated by Andreas J. Köstenberger. 2nd ed. Grand Rapids: Baker, 1999.

Stanton, Graham. *Jesus and Gospel.* Cambridge: Cambridge University Press, 2004.

Thielman, Frank. *Theology of the New Testament: A Canonical and Synthetic Approach.* Grand Rapids: Zondervan, 2005.

Turner, Max. *The Holy Spirit and Spiritual Gifts: Then and Now.* Carlisle, Cumbria: Paternoster, 1996.

Williams, Rowan. *Resurrection: Interpreting the Easter Gospel.* 2nd ed. London: Darton, Longman & Todd, 2002.

———. *Tokens of Trust: An Introduction to Christian Belief.* Louisville: Westminster John Knox, 2007.

Wright, N. T. *The Challenge of Jesus: Rediscovering Who Jesus Was and Is.* Downers Grove, IL: InterVarsity, 1999.

———. *Jesus and the Victory of God.* Vol. 2 of *Christian Origins and the Question of God.* Minneapolis: Fortress, 1996.

———. *The New Testament and the People of God.* Vol. 1 of *Christian Origins and the Question of God.* Minneapolis: Fortress, 1992.

———. *The Resurrection of the Son of God.* Vol. 3 of *Christian Origins and the Question of God.* Minneapolis: Fortress, 2003.

———. *Simply Christian: Why Christianity Makes Sense.* San Francisco: HarperSanFrancisco, 2006.

———. *Surprised by Hope: Rethinking Heaven, the Resurrection, and the Mission of the Church.* New York: HarperOne, 2008.

Scripture Index

Subject Index

anthropology. *See* humanity.
apostles, 13, 19, 46–47, 77, 80,
 82–83, 98, 101, 110
atonement, 21–22, 27, 30, 55,
 89, 100, 110. *See also*
 Jesus, death of.

baptism, 56–57, 100, 110
Bible. *See* Scripture.
bibliology. *See* Scripture.

Christology. *See* Jesus.
church,
 nature and purpose of the,
 85, 93–95, 98–100,
 104, 108, 111
 unity and diversity of the,
 95–101, 103
Communion. *See* Eucharist.
covenant,
 new, 18, 23–24, 27, 48, 50,
 55, 74–77, 82–83, 89,
 98, 111
 through Moses, 6, 22–24,
 37, 61–62, 111, 114, 116
 with Abraham, 61–62, 111

creation, 20, 32–34, 36, 41, 47,
 54–55, 59–61, 64–66,
 81, 85–88, 93, 95, 100,
 102–3. *See also* new
 creation.
creed,
 Apostles', 99, 105, 107–8
 "gospel," 1–2, 19, 46–47,
 53, 80
 Nicene, 99
crucifixion. *See* Jesus, death of.

death, 5–7, 20–21, 26–27,
 42, 53, 55, 86–89, 91,
 93–94. *See also* sin.

ecclesiology. *See* church.
ethics, 24–26, 29–30, 78–79,
 90–91, 103
eschatology, 6, 12, 15, 34,
 74–75, 77, 86, 99, 104,
 109–12, 114, 116
Eucharist, 24, 56–57, 112
evil powers, 26–27, 54–55,
 109. *See also* sin.
exile, 23, 38, 47–51, 75